Learning and Mastering Medical Terminology, Block 3

Career Step, LLC
Phone: 801.489.9393
Toll-Free: 800.246.7837
Fax: 801.491.6645
careerstep.com

This text companion contains a snapshot of the online program content converted to a printed format. Please note that the online training program is constantly changing and improving and is always the source of the most up-to-date information.

Product Number: HG-PR-11-034
Generation Date: February 16, 2012

Table of Contents

Unit 1
Introduction

> ## *Learning Objective*
> In this module, the student will learn about medical plurals, medical slang and jargon, foreign medical terms, word differentiation, and medical abbreviations. A review of the previous Learning and Mastering Medical Terminology modules will also be presented.

You've worked your way through the basic building blocks of medical terminology—A through Z. Medical language, like any language, has singular/plural forms, add-ons, special rules, exceptions, and an unofficial or "slang" version. This module will take you through rules, examples, and some common medical jargon.

Here are some slang expressions that you may have heard before.

- When pigs fly
- The apple of my eye
- Pull someone's leg
- Spill the beans

That's the Cat's Meow

Unit 2
Plurals

Plurals – Introduction

If one is good, two is better! Right? Not always, but fortunately the language of medicine takes into account that body parts are not always singular.

One very important skill required for understanding and using the language of medicine is a working knowledge of medical plurals. You'll find it helpful to be able to recognize the plural form of many terms with which you may not presently be familiar.

Plurals Rules

There are *general* as well as *specific* rules for forming plurals in the English language. The general rules are described later in this module. However, as medical words are (for the most part) of Latin and Greek origins, the rules for pluralization can be more complex than are the rules for forming plurals in English.

Medical Plurals

Open any dictionary (or pull up any dictionary site on the Internet) and look up the word *crux*. You will see the entry contains the following information:

Crux (kruks) pl. cruces [L.] cross

The word is Crux, pronounced "kruks."

The plural of the crux is cruces.

The Latin root word is cross.

Most dictionaries handle plurals in medical language in a similar fashion.

You must be CAREFUL to note the way a plural word is used in a medical document; plural rules are sometimes applied incorrectly and can lead to unclear meaning. You will want to always remember to consider terminology in context and, when necessary, seek clarification.

> **Example:**
>
> Fingers and toes are called *phalanges*. This is the plural form of the word *phalanx*, which is used when referring to only one finger or toe. However, medical practitioners will sometimes refer to a single finger or toe as a "phalange." If you see the word *phalange* in a medical report, it should raise a red flag—since *phalange* is not a real word. You must determine if the report refers to *phalanges* (several fingers or toes) or a single *phalanx* (one finger or one toe).

Finally, keep in mind these rules probably made a lot of sense to the ancient Romans. You undoubtedly have an intuitive feel for English plurals, but medical plurals follow the rules of Latin and will not feel so familiar.

Plurals – Rules 1-3

There are three basic English rules about forming plurals. You learned these in school and use them in your everyday language. Consequently, they are reviewed here only briefly for your reference.

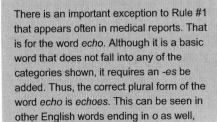

There is an important exception to Rule #1 that appears often in medical reports. That is for the word *echo*. Although it is a basic word that does not fall into any of the categories shown, it requires an *-es* be added. Thus, the correct plural form of the word *echo* is *echoes*. This can be seen in other English words ending in *o* as well, such as *potato* and *tomato*.

Plural Rule #1: *For most words, simply add an -s to the end of the word.*

EXAMPLES: sample = samples, bed = beds, specimen = specimens, pill = pills, doctor = doctors, hospital = hospitals

Plural Rule #2: *For words ending in -s, -z, -ch, -sh (and nonmedical -x) add an -es to the end of the word.*

EXAMPLES: dish = dishes, lunch = lunches, loss = losses, reflex = reflexes

Plural Rule #3: *For words ending in -y which are preceded by a consonant, change the -y to an i and add -es. (For words ending in -y preceded by a vowel simply add an -s, i.e., plays, monkeys.)*

EXAMPLES: allergy = allergies, anomaly = anomalies, body = bodies, abnormality = abnormalities, party = parties

I. **FILL IN THE BLANK.**
   Enter the correct plural form of the word in the space provided.

1. search _____   2. history _____

3. avulsion _____   4. extremity _____

5. calcification _____ 6. church _____

7. cytology _____   8. day _____

9. emergency _____   10. fracture _____

11. duty _____   12. trauma _____

13. boss _____   14. blush _____

15. angiography _____   16. echo _____

17. leukocyte _____   18. stitch _____

19. peduncle _____   20. theology _____

Plurals – Rule 4

Plural Rule #4: *For words ending in -um change the -um to an -a.*

EXAMPLES: antrum = antra, ostium = ostia, velum = vela, ischium = ischia, diverticulum = diverticula.

NOTE: One of life's great certainties is that language constantly changes. Be aware that, although you are learning the standard Latin medical plurals, the fact is that many dictators simply add an *s*. Generally, it is all right to put the word they dictate: *antrums, stromas, ganglions, craniums, leiomyomas*. In addition, as with many grammatical issues, there are exceptions to almost every rule.

I. FILL IN THE BLANK.

Following are words that require use of the above rule for making them plural. In the space provided, enter the plural form of each word.

1. acetabulum _____

2. antrum _____

3. brachium _____

4. capitulum _____

5. cavum _____

6. cilium _____

7. coccidium _____

8. cranium _____

9. diverticulum _____

10. dorsum _____

11. endometrium _____

12. endothelium _____

13. epithelium _____

14. frenulum _____

15. haustrum _____

16. hilum _____

17. infundibulum _____

18. ischium _____

19. labium _____

20. labrum _____

21. mediastinum _____

22. omentum _____

23. ostium _____

24. planum _____

25. pudendum _____

26. retinaculum _____

27. rostrum _____

28. spatium _____

29. spectrum _____

30. speculum _____

31. stratum _____

32. tegmentum _____

33. tentorium _____

34. tuberculum _____

35. reticulum _____

Plurals – Rule 5

Plural Rule #5: For words that end in -a, add an -e.

EXAMPLES: bursa = bursae, lingula = lingulae, uvula = uvulae

There is an important exception to this rule for words ending in -oma or -gma such as stroma. In this instance, add the letters -ta to the end of the word (stromata). Other examples of this are stigma = stigmata, leiomyoma = leiomyomata.

Another exception is in the following two words. These words appear only as plural forms: *adnexa* and *genitalia*. These should be treated as plurals in grammatical usage. "Genitalia are normal." (not "is") There are singular forms, but you will never see or hear them.

I. FILL IN THE BLANK.
Following are words that require use of the above rule for making them plural. In the space provided, enter the plural form of each word.

1. adnexa _____

2. uvula _____

3. fascia _____

4. stoma _____

5. trochlea _____

6. vagina _____

7. medulla _____

8. vertebra _____

9. condyloma _____

10. petechia _____

11. vallecula _____

12. ampulla _____

13. synechia _____

14. plica _____

15. porta _____

16. leiomyoma _____

17. stria _____

18. lingua _____

19. genitalia _____

20. sequela _____

21. bulla _____

22. scatoma _____

23. areola _____

24. conjunctiva _____

25. sella _____

26. stroma _____

27. vesicula _____

28. aura _____

29. concha _____

30. sclera _____

Plurals – Rule 6

Plural Rule #6: *For words ending in -us, replace the -us with a single -i.*

EXAMPLES: lobus = lobi, tragus = tragi, focus = foci

There are exceptions to this rule as well.

First, there are two words you should memorize, *meatus* and *plexus*. Their plural and singular forms are exactly the same. Grammatically, they are treated as singular forms. "The solar plexus is tender to palpation."

Second, there are three unusual exceptions, all ending in *-us*. These are: *viscus* which becomes *viscera*; *crus* which becomes *crura*; and *corpus* which becomes *corpora*. You should memorize these exceptions.

I. FILL IN THE BLANK.
Following are words that require use of the above rule for making them plural. In the space provided, enter the plural form of each word.

1. stimulus _____

2. alveolus _____

3. annulus _____

4. viscus _____

5. malleolus _____

6. ramus _____

7. meatus _____

8. truncus _____

9. humerus _____

10. panniculus _____

11. crus _____

12. glomerulus _____

13. globus _____

14. limbus _____

15. vagus _____

16. uterus _____

17. corpus _____

18. meniscus _____

19. thrombus _____

20. fundus _____

21. nevus _____

22. canaliculus _____

23. plexus _____

24. bronchus _____

25. calculus _____

26. sulcus _____

27. bacillus _____

28. talus _____

29. villus _____

30. tophus _____

Plurals – Rules 7-8

Plural Rule #7: For words ending in -en, change the -en to -ina.

EXAMPLES: foramen = foramina, lumen = lumina

This is an uncommon ending; be sure to note the examples above.

Plural Rule #8: In words ending in -is, change the -i to an -e.

EXAMPLES: metastasis = metastases, naris = nares, pelvis = pelves

There are exceptions to this rule as well. These, although uniform, are unusual exceptions and should be memorized individually. They are: *arthritis*, which becomes *arthritides*; *cuspis*, which becomes *cuspides*; and *iris*, which becomes *irides*.

I. FILL IN THE BLANK.
Following are words that require use of the above rules for making them plural. In the space provided, enter the plural form of each word.

1. ankylosis _____   2. testis _____

3. iris _____   4. paralysis _____

5. epiphysis _____   6. diuresis _____

7. arthritis _____   8. prosthesis _____

9. pubis _____   10. anastomosis _____

11. diaphysis _____   12. metastasis _____

13. cuspis _____   14. synchondrosis _____

15. aponeurosis _____

Plurals – Rule 9

Plural Rule #9: **In words ending in either -ex or -ix, the ending is replaced with -ices.**

An exception to the rule is the word **reflex**. *The only acceptable plural is* **reflexes**.

EXAMPLES: cervix = cervices, apex = apices, vertex = vertices

If any other letter precedes the -x in the word (with the exception of -n), simply replace the -x with -ces.

EXAMPLES: falx = falces, thorax = thoraces

Finally, if the -x is preceded by the letter -n, replace the -x with -ges.

EXAMPLES: pharynx = pharynges, phalanx = phalanges

I. FILL IN THE BLANK.
Following are words that require use of the above rule for making them plural. In the space provided, enter the plural form of each word.

1. appendix _____   2. vortex _____

3. crux _____   4. larynx _____

5. calix _____   6. thorax _____

7. index _____   8. falx _____

9. apex _____   10. matrix _____

11. cicatrix _____   12. phalanx _____

13. varix _____   14. cervix _____

15. vertex _____

Review: Plurals

I. **FILL IN THE BLANK.**
   Enter the correct plural form of the word in the blank provided.

1. bronchus _____   2. echo _____

3. labrum _____   4. torus _____

5. adnexa _____   6. lamella _____

7. appendix _____   8. viscus _____

9. branch _____   10. reticulum _____

11. corpus _____   12. tegmentum _____

13. mamma _____   14. condyloma _____

15. chemistry _____   16. fistula _____

17. falx _____   18. arthritis _____

19. panniculus _____   20. cicatrix _____

21. metaphysis _____   22. maxilla _____

23. meatus _____   24. foramen _____

25. speculum _____   26. iris _____

27. humerus _____   28. cervix _____

29. lumen _____   30. spectrum _____

31. apophysis _____   32. sulcus _____

33. phalanx _____   34. malleolus _____

35. pelvis _____   36. ramus _____

37. plexus _____

38. synechia _____

39. prosthesis _____

40. baby _____

Plurals Rules and Exceptions

With your study of prefixes, suffixes, root words, and plurals, you have developed a strong basic medical language vocabulary. Your study, of course, does not include every word you will come across in medical reports, but you are laying a solid foundation for getting started.

Keep your dictionary handy as you review the plural rules and exceptions—it's your best friend for verifying and double-checking!

Rules	Examples	
	Singular	Plural
Add an *s* to the end of the word	doctor	doctors
Words ending in *s, z, ch*, and *sh*, add an *es* to the end of the word	loss	losses
Words ending in *y* preceded by a consonant, change the *y* to an *i* and add *es*	anomaly	anomalies
words ending in *y* preceded by a vowel, add an *s*	play	plays
Words ending in *um*, change to an *a*	ischium	ischia
Words ending in *a*, add an *e*	uvula	uvulae
Words ending in *us*, replace with a single *i*	focus	foci
Words ending in *en*, change the *en* to *ina*	lumen	lumina
Words ending in *is*, change the *i* to an *e*	pelvis	pelves
Words ending in *ex* or *ix*, replace the ending with *ices*	cervix	cervices
If any other letter precedes the *x* in the word (with the exception of *n*), simply replace the *x* with *ces*	thorax	thoraces
If the *x* is preceded by the letter *n*, replace the *x* with *ges*	phalanx	phalanges

The following is a list of the exceptions to the plural rules.

Exceptions	Examples	
	Singular	Plural
Add an *es* to the end of the word instead of an *s*	echo	echoes
Words ending in *oma* or *gma*, add the letters *ta* to the end of the word	stigma	stigmata
Plural form only	none	adnexa
	none	genitalia
The plural and singular forms are the same	meatus	meatus
	plexus	plexus

Words ending in *us*	viscus	viscera
	crus	crura
	corpus	corpora
Words ending in *is*	arthritis	arthritides
	cuspis	cuspides
	iris	irides
Words ending in *ex*	reflex	reflexes

Unit 3
Slang and Jargon

Slang and Jargon – Introduction

The word *slang* is defined as as:

"…very informal usage in vocabulary and idiom that is characteristically more metaphorical, playful, elliptical, vivid, and ephemeral than ordinary language." *

Slang is part of everyday language, and it is also part of medical language. In fact, practitioners of medical language use slang, jargon, or shortened forms so often some slang/jargon terms become commonly accepted medical terminology. These terms are not even recognized as slang anymore because they have become so commonplace. However, most slang terms don't ever reach acceptable status and, as stated above, are "short-lived and…. considered unsuitable."

Although less formal than the medical language you have studied thus far, slang, jargon, and shortened forms are still a part of the language of medical reports. You will encounter this less formal language in the medical records you review and code, and you need to be able to recognize it.

Slang, jargon, and shortened forms may not provide enough clarity of meaning to accurately assign medical codes. You may need to seek additional information or ask for clarification when slang, jargon, or shortened forms in medical documents prevent accurate and complete coding of the medical record.

> **Highlights**
>
> Slang terms and phrases (English or medical language slang) should be avoided in medical documents to ensure clarity, accuracy, and legal integrity.

Slang and jargon will appear in medical records, particularly in clinic notes, nurses' notes, and other more casual medical documents. You will sometimes find yourself exposed to it and coding it, so let's take a look at slang and jargon.

(*Dictionary.com Unabridged, version 1.1.. http://dictionary.reference.com/browse/slang.)

Slang and Jargon in Healthcare Documentation

Before you begin studying common slang, jargon, and short terms, let's take just a minute to look at the big picture with regard to healthcare documentation involving slang and jargon.

Many medical reports are legal documents, and they should be comprehensible to judges and juries. Medical terminology that appears in medical dictionaries and medical references can be deciphered—even when it's complex and technical. Figuring out the meaning when terms are non-standard and not precisely defined can be difficult, if not impossible. A clear record using standard English and standard medical language protects patient and healthcare provider.

> **Highlights**
>
> You may need to seek additional information or ask for clarification when slang, jargon, or shortened forms in medical documents prevent accurate and complete coding of the medical record.

Along those same lines, adult patients and the parents of children under medical care must be able to understand, insofar as possible, the language in the reports concerning themselves and their children. Making informed decisions, evaluating treatment options, obtaining consultative medical care with different providers, and other healthcare decisions are all made easier with clear medical record documentation.

The purpose of the healthcare documentation process is to create an understandable, accurate record of patient care. Slang, jargon, and short forms have a place in medical records, just like in everyday life, but used excessively they can undermine the healthcare documentation process and impact quality of patient care.

Let's switch over from the dark side! It's not all bad. Slang/jargon is part of medical language and many slang/jargon terms and short forms have been adopted as a very acceptable part of medical language. The next several lessons will give you the chance to study and review some common slang, jargon, and short forms.

Slang and Jargon – Lesson 1

I. **TERMINOLOGY.**
    Enter the formal term in the space provided. Read the definition and description for each term.

1. **a-fib, A-fib, or AFib** _____
Atrial fibrillation (a severe cardiac arrhythmia).

2. **alk phos** _____
Alkaline phosphatase (a lab value for a chemical in the blood).

3. **appy** _____
Appendectomy or appendicitis (excision of the appendix or infection/inflammation of the appendix).

4. **bicarb** _____
Bicarbonate (one of the electrolytes, with sodium, potassium, and chloride).

5. **bili** _____
Bilirubin (a lab value for liver function testing).

6. **CBC with diff** _____
CBC (complete blood count) with differential (the percentages of different types of white cells in the blood).

7. **caps** _____
Capsules (a form of medications).

8. **cath** _____
Catheter or catheterization (a tube or the placement of tubes in the body).

9. **chemo** _____
Chemotherapy (treatment with chemical compounds, usually referring to cancer regimens).

10. **chole** _____
Cholecystectomy (excision of the gallbladder).

II. MATCHING.
Match the correct term to the definition.

1. ____ A tube or the placement of tubes in the body.

2. ____ A severe cardiac arrhythmia.

3. ____ Excision of the appendix or inflammation of the appendix.

4. ____ Treatment with chemical compounds.

5. ____ A chemical in the blood.

6. ____ Excision of the gallbladder.

7. ____ A lab value for liver function.

8. ____ A form of medication.

9. ____ Percentages of different types of white blood cells.

10. ____ One of the electrolytes.

A. cholecystectomy
B. chemotherapy
C. complete blood count with differential
D. atrial fibrillation
E. bicarbonate
F. catheter or catheterization
G. appendectomy or appendicitis
H. bilirubin
I. alkaline phosphatase
J. capsules

Slang and Jargon – Lesson 2

I. TERMINOLOGY.
Enter the formal term in the space provided. Read the definition and description for each term.

1. **crit** _____

Hematocrit (test for packed red cells in the blood).

2. **DC** _____

Discontinue or discharge, past tense DC'd, sometimes dc/dc'd (acceptable in a clinic or nurse's note but not in a formal document).

3. **detox** _____

Detoxification (treatment for acute alcohol abuse or other drug overuse).

4. **dig** _____

Digoxin or digitalis; pronounced wih a short i and g sounding like j (medication for cardiac problems).

5. **dip sesta** _____

Dipyridamole sestamibi (a nuclear x-ray exam).

6. **double J stent** _____

JJ stent (a surgical device for keeping tubes in place).

7. **echo** _____

Echocardiogram (recording of heart function by analyzing sound waves).

8. **eos** _____

Eosinophils (white blood cells that are part of the CBC with differential).

9. **exam** _____

Examination (evaluation, as in physical examination or Mental Status Examination).

10. **flex sig** _____

Flexible sigmoidoscopy (inspection of the sigmoid, the S-shaped lower portion of the colon, with a flexible endoscopic instrument).

II. MATCHING.
Match the correct term to the definition.

1. ____ Treatment for acute alcohol abuse or other drug overuse.

2. ____ White blood cells.

3. ____ Evaluation.

4. ____ Inspection of the sigmoid with a flexible endoscopic instrument.

5. ____ Recording of heart function by analyzing sound waves.

6. ____ DC—acceptable in a nurse's note.

7. ____ Medication for cardiac problems.

8. ____ Surgical device for keeping tubes in place.

9. ____ A nuclear x-ray exam.

10. ____ A test for packed red blood cells.

A. flexible sigmoidoscopy
B. dipyridamole sestamibi
C. digoxin or digitalis
D. eosinophils
E. detoxification
F. JJ stent
G. hematocrit
H. examination
I. discontinue or discharge
J. echocardiogram

Slang and Jargon – Lesson 3

I. TERMINOLOGY.
Enter the formal term in the space provided. Read the definition and description for each term.

1. **Foley** _____

Foley catheter (a catheter commonly used during surgical procedures for draining urine from the bladder).

2. **HCTZ** _____

Hydrochlorothiazide (a medication for the control of hypertension and edema).

3. **hem/onc** _____

Hematology/oncology (the medical specialty that deals with cancer and blood problems).

4. **hep C (A, B)** _____

Hepatitis C (A, B) (liver disease characterized by infection and inflammation).

5. **K** _____

Potassium (the chemical symbol for the element potassium. This is an acceptable usage.)

6. **KCl** _____

Potassium chloride (the chemical formula for potassium chloride; it is often given to cardiac patients whose potassium is depleted by diuretic medications, such as Lasix. This is an acceptable usage.)

7. **lac** _____

Laceration (a cut produced by trauma).

8. **lymphs** _____

Lymphocytes (another type of white blood cell included in the CBC with differential).

9. **lytes** _____

Electrolytes (usually sodium, potassium, chloride, and bicarbonate; they are blood chemistries evaluated in laboratory studies).

10. **mag** _____

Magnesium (a chemical in the blood, also a medication given for some medical conditions, such as alcohol overdose).

II. MATCHING.
Match the correct term to the definition.

1. ____ Liver disease characterized by infection and inflammation.

2. ____ A catheter commonly used during surgical procedures for draining urine from the bladder.

3. ____ Sodium, potassium, chloride, and bicarbonate, blood chemistries evaluated in laboratory studies.

4. ____ A cut produced by trauma.

5. ____ A chemical in the blood, also a medication given for some medical conditions, such as alcohol overdose.

6. ____ The expanded name for the chemical KCl.

7. ____ The medical specialty that deals with cancer and blood problems.

8. ____ Another type of white blood cell included in the CBC with differential.

9. ____ K is the chemical symbol for this element.

10. ____ A medication for the control of hypertension and edema.

A. laceration
B. potassium
C. hepatitis
D. hematology and oncology
E. Foley catheter
F. hydrochlorothiazide
G. potassium chloride
H. electrolytes
I. lymphocytes
J. magnesium

Slang and Jargon – Lesson 4

I. TERMINOLOGY.
Enter the formal term in the space provided. Read the definition and description for each term.

1. **meds** _____

Medications (drugs given to patients; pharmacopeia).

2. **mets** _____

Metastases, singular met/metastasis (the spread of malignant neoplasm—cancer—from the primary site to one or more secondary sites).

3. **migs** _____

Milligrams, written as mg (metric unit of measurement, the most common form of drug dosage).

4. **mikes** _____

Micrograms, written as mcg (metric unit of measurement smaller than the milligram, also used in some drug dosages).

5. **monos** _____

Monocytes (white blood cells that are a part of the CBC with differential).

6. **nebs** _____

Nebulizers (an aerated form of medications given for pulmonary problems such as asthma).

7. **neuro** _____

Neurological or neurology (referring to the medical specialty or to the part of the physical exam that evaluates neurologic or central nervous system function).

8. **neuropsych** _____

Neuropsychiatric or neuropsychiatry (pertaining to the study of the combination of neurology and psychiatry—often related, since both study brain function).

9. **O2 sat** _____

Oxygen saturation (the amount of oxygen present in the blood; measured by pulse oximetry).

10. **path** _____

Pathology (the study of the essential nature of disease, particularly as it relates to changes in tissues, organs, etc. Also the cause of disease).

II. MATCHING.
Match the definition to the appropriate term.

1. ____ The amount of oxygen present in the blood.

2. ____ Metric units of measurement, the most common form of drug dosage.

3. ____ The study of the essential nature of disease.

4. ____ An aerated form of medications given for pulmonary problems such as asthma.

5. ____ Pertaining to the study of two related medical specialties.

6. ____ Drugs.

7. ____ Metric unit of measurement smaller than the milligram.

8. ____ The spread of cancer from a primary to a secondary site.

9. ____ A part of the physical examination or the study of nerve function.

10. ____ A type of white blood cell.

A. pathology
B. nebulizers
C. medications
D. micrograms
E. metastases
F. monocytes
G. oxygen saturation
H. milligrams
I. neuropsychiatric
J. neurology or neurological

Slang and Jargon – Lesson 5

I. **TERMINOLOGY.**
   Enter the formal term in the space provided. Read the definition and description for each term.

1. **perf** _____

Perforation (a hole, as in a perforated eardrum or perforated bowel).

2. **preop** _____

Preoperative (before an operation). Occasionally, but rarely, a dictator will use the term "preopped" (alternative spelling "preopp'd"). This is not really a short form for anything that can reasonably be expanded without rewriting the sentence. It is an example of a slang/jargon term that "more accurately communicates meaning" than any possible expansion of it would.

3. **postop** _____

Postoperative (after an operation).

4. **prepped** _____

Prepared (a short form commonly used in surgical reports; e.g., "The patient was prepped and draped").

5. **psych** _____

Psychiatry, psychology (the specialties that address the mind and mental processes).

6. **pulse ox** _____

Pulse oximetry (the process of determining oxygen saturation by use of machine measurements).

7. **regurg** _____

Regurgitation (flow in the opposite direction from normal, as in vomiting stomach contents or backward flow of the blood through vascular structures).

8. **rehab** _____

Rehabilitation (the process of restoring normal form and function after injury or illness by means of physical, psychosocial, vocational, or recreational activities).

9. **sat** _____

Saturation (a measure of the degree to which oxygen is bound to the hemoglobin in the blood; it is given as a percentage, and reflects pulmonary function).

II. MATCHING.
Match the correct term to the definition.

1. ____ The process of restoring normal form and function.

2. ____ The means of measuring oxygen saturation.

3. ____ The specialties that address the mind and mental processes.

4. ____ Before an operation.

5. ____ The degree to which oxygen in the blood is bound to hemoglobin.

6. ____ Short form commonly used in surgical reports with "draped."

7. ____ Following surgery.

8. ____ Flow in the opposite direction from normal.

9. ____ A hole.

A. preoperative
B. psychology/psychiatry
C. postoperative
D. regurgitation
E. saturation
F. pulse oximetry
G. prepared
H. rehabilitation
I. perforation

Slang and Jargon – Lesson 6

I. TERMINOLOGY.
Enter the formal term in the space provided. Read the definition and description for each term.

1. **sed rate** _____

Sedimentation rate (a laboratory value related to the action of red blood cells).

2. **segs** _____

Segmented neutrophils (white blood cells that are part of the CBC differential).

3. **t. bili** _____

Total bilirubin (a bile pigment that is measured in liver function studies).

4. **tabs** _____

Tablets (a form of medication, pills).

5. **triple A** _____

Abdominal aortic aneurysm (AAA, a cardiovascular anomaly).

6. **V-tach** _____

Ventricular tachycardia (an increased ventricular heart rate).

7. **voc rehab** _____

Vocational rehabilitation (rehabilitation for those who need to retrain in a former or new vocation due to illness or injury).

II. **MATCHING.**
   Match the correct term to the definition.

   1. ____ An increased ventricular heart rate.

   2. ____ Retraining for a new or former vocation.

   3. ____ A laboratory value related to the action of red blood cells.

   4. ____ White blood cells that are part of the CBC differential.

   5. ____ A form of medication.

   6. ____ A cardiovascular anomaly of the aorta.

   7. ____ A bile pigment measured in liver function studies.

   A. sedimentation rate
   B. total bilirubin
   C. abdominal aortic aneurysm
   D. ventricular tachycardia
   E. segmented neutrophils
   F. vocational rehabilitation
   G. tablets

Unit 4
Foreign Terms

Foreign Terms – Introduction

As you have already learned, most medical words come into English from Latin and Greek. Some of them, like medical plurals, even bring the Latin and/or Greek grammar rules with them. You have been exposed to some of these already:

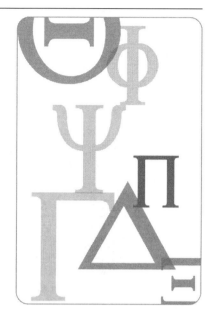

- *condyloma* becomes *condylomata*
- *adnexus* becomes *adnexa* (in fact, you never see that particular word in the singular)
- *diverticulum* becomes *diverticula*
- *apex* becomes *apices*
- *corpus* becomes *corpora*

Often, over time, as the words are more widely used, the Latin plurals will gradually disappear from common usage: the plural of *ganglion* is equally acceptable as *ganglia* (Latin plural) and *ganglions* (English plural).

For the most part, however, this change has not occurred, so you must learn the rules for plurals, as well as other Latin and Greek forms. Terms like *chondromalacia patellae*, *pruritus vulvae*, and *abruptio placentae* represent the possessive forms of the Latin terms: chondromalacia of the patella, itching of the vulva, and abruption of the placenta.

Fortunately for you, in the workplace where you are using medical terminology, you simply have to be able to identify a term without having to know Latin grammar. (And aren't you HAPPY about that?)

Foreign terms are often introduced into English usage without undergoing any changes to standardize the term with other medical usage. The medical vocabulary simply includes such terms in their natural non-English form, and they are often pronounced with non-English pronunciations.

Not only does the vocabulary of medicine incorporate such terms, but legal vocabulary does as well: *pro bono*, *per annum*, *a priori*, *non sequitur*. These terms, and many others like them, are not at all uncommon in English conversation and writing.

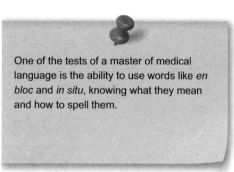

One of the tests of a master of medical language is the ability to use words like *en bloc* and *in situ*, knowing what they mean and how to spell them.

The following lessons introduce you to such terms. These are presented, along with their abbreviations and their definitions, with an occasional instance which demonstrates how they are used. The list is by no means exhaustive, but is intended as a good basic introduction.

Foreign Terms – Lesson 1

Learn these terms, and similar ones should come easy to you when you run across them.

Note: Most of the abbreviated forms of these terms are okay with or without periods: AD or A.D., AS or A.S., OD or O.D., OS or O.S., for example.

I. TERMINOLOGY.
Enter each term in the space provided. Read the definition and description for each term.

1. **addendum** _____

Things to be added. Plural is addenda (or addendums; both are acceptable English usage, but addenda is preferred.).

2. **ad libitum** _____

Shortened to ad lib. According to your pleasure. "The patient is to resume activity ad lib."

3. **auris dextra** _____

A.D., right ear.

4. **auris sinistra** _____

A.S., left ear. Did you know that the word *sinister* comes from the term that means "left-handed"?

5. **aures utrae** _____

A.U., each ear (often interpreted as "both ears").

6. **bruit(s)** _____

Pronounced broo-ee(s). This is an abnormal vascular sound heard on auscultation during a physical exam. Look it up in your dictionary and you will see that nearly all the different types of bruits are French terms.

7. **cafe au lait spot** _____

This is a skin lesion that is the color of coffee with milk—a distinctive light brown pigment having a macular form. Pronounced "kahFAY o LAY."

8. **coup** _____

A hit or stroke; found in such terms as coup de grace (coo day grawss), coup d'etat (coo day taw), contrecoup (contray-coo—as in a certain kind of brain injury).

9. **cul-de-sac** _____

A blind alley. Usually has reference to the uterine cul-de-sac.

II. FILL IN THE BLANK.
Use terms and not abbreviations in your answers. Some answers may require more than one word to be complete.

1. Coffee-colored. _____

2. Right ear. _____

3. Added thing. _____

4. Blind alley, as the uterus. _____

5. AS or A.S. _____

6. At your pleasure. _____

7. A hit or stroke. _____

8. Both ears or each ear. _____

9. Abnormal sound. _____

Foreign Terms – Lesson 2

I. TERMINOLOGY.
Enter each term in the space provided. Read the definition and description for each term.

1. **en bloc** _____

In one block. Common term in surgery and pathology where a specimen is removed in one piece. It is pronounced "on block." But don't get it wrong by spelling it that way!

2. **en masse** _____

In mass—sometimes refers to one unit, not divided into parts. Pronounced "on mass" or sometimes "on moss."

3. **Gilbert disease** _____

Pronounced zhee-BEAR. An inborn abnormality of liver function.

4. **in ano** _____

About the only place you will ever hear this is in reference to "fistula in ano," which is an abnormal opening near the anus.

5. **in extremis** _____

At the point of death.

6. **in situ** _____

In its original position; in its natural or normal place. "The carcinoma in situ has not spread to surrounding tissues." Very common term in pathology reports.

7. **in toto** _____

As a whole or in the whole, a totality. "The specimen was removed in toto."

II. FILL IN THE BLANK.
   Use terms and not abbreviations in your answers. Some answers may require more than one word to be complete.

1. Liver function disease. _____   2. Not divided into parts. _____

3. In its original position. _____   4. Totality. _____

5. In a block. _____   6. Near the anus. _____

7. At the point of death. _____

Foreign Terms – Lesson 3

I. TERMINOLOGY.
   Enter each term in the space provided. Read the definition and description for each term.

1. **oculus dexter** _____

O.D., right eye.

2. **oculus sinister** _____

O.S., left eye.

3. **oculus uterque** _____

O.U., each eye. Again, you will often hear the abbreviations for these terms, but will rarely, if ever, hear the words themselves.

4. **peau d'orange** _____

pronounced "po-dranzh." Literally means "orange peel" and describes the appearance of the skin in certain dermatological conditions.

5. **per** _____

For, through, by. Per diem, by the day. Millimeters per second. Per annum, by the year.

6. **raphe** _____

Pronounced "rah-fay." It is included here because of its unusual pronunciation. Literally the word means "seam" and refers to the line of union between various symmetrical physiologic structures.

7. **Raynaud phenomenon or disease** _____

Pronounced "ray-NO." This is a vascular disorder characterized by intermittent loss of circulation, usually to the extremities.

8. **statim** _____

At once, immediately. You will hear this as "stat."

9. **status quo** _____

The existing condition. "There was no change in the patient's status quo."

10. **Virchow-Robin spaces** _____

Pronounced "ver-cow ro-BAN." A perivascular space in the brain in which important immunological functions take place.

II. **FILL IN THE BLANK.**
Use terms and not abbreviations in your answers. Some answers may require more than one word to be complete.

1. Through or by. _____

2. Immediately. _____

3. Orange peel. _____

4. A seam. _____

5. A space in the brain. _____

6. The existing condition. _____

7. Right eye. _____

8. OS or O.S. _____

9. Vascular phenomenon. _____

10. Each eye or both eyes. _____

Foreign Terms – Lesson 4

The next two lessons introduce you to terms that are used in medication dosage instructions. Of note, much of this information will be review for you. These foreign terms are different from most of the ones in this unit because you will rarely, if ever, see them spelled out in context, whatever the context. The abbreviations for them are very commonly used in medical reports, in prescription writing, and in other applications. They are presented here in the classical, formal abbreviation style, such as should be used in legal medical documents (like hospital discharge summaries, consultations, operation reports, etc.). In clinic notes, nurses' notes, other chart notes, prescriptions, and other less formal settings, the periods are often left out of the abbreviated forms: qid, bid, prn, ac, or q4h, for example.

It is important to note that there is considerable variation in the actual dictation of drug dosage instructions and consequently in the transcription of drug dosages as well. Dictators may use the Latin abbreviations, occasional English abbreviations, a mixture of Latin and English abbreviations, or no abbreviations at all (e.g., the dictator may say "q.d," "daily," "q. daily," "once a day," or "every day").

I. **TERMINOLOGY.**
Enter each term in the space provided. Read the definition and description for each term.

1. **ante cibum** _____

a.c. Before food. "Medication to be taken 40 mg a.c."

2. **ante meridiem** _____

a.m. In the morning. "He will be seen at 10:00 a.m. in the morning"—is totally redundant. Correct it if you see or hear it. The abbreviation a.m. is common in drug dosages. AM is also an acceptable form.

3. **bis in die** _____

b.i.d. Twice a day or twice daily.

4. **die** _____

d. Day. This is the "d" in most abbreviations.

5. **gutta** _____

g.t.t. A drop. Often appears in medication lists in reference to eardrops or eyedrops.

6. **hora** _____

h. Hour. "Amoxicillin 500 mg q.4h. or q. 4 h."

7. **hora somni** _____

h.s. At bedtime (literally the hour of sleep). "She was to take her Elavil q.h.s."

8. **per os** _____

p.o. By mouth. "Lasix 40 p.o. q.d."

II. **FILL IN THE BLANK.**
Enter the English translation of the following terms. Some answers may require more than one word to be complete.

1. hora _____   2. b.i.d. _____

3. p.o. _____   4. h.s. _____

5. a.c. _____   6. die _____

7. gutta _____   8. a.m. _____

Foreign Terms – Lesson 5

I. **TERMINOLOGY.**
Enter each term in the space provided. Read the definition and description for each term.

1. **post meridiem** _____

p.m. Afternoon, or between noon and midnight.

2. **pro re nata** _____

p.r.n. As needed. "Tylenol 325 mg q.4h. p.r.n. pain."

3. **quaque die** _____

q.d. Every day.

4. **quaque hora** _____

q.h. Every hour.

5. **quaque secunda hora** _____

Abbreviated q.2h. This means every 2 hours.

6. **quaque tertia hora** _____

q.3h. Every 3 hours.

7. **quaque quarta hora** _____

q.4h. Every 4 hours.

8. **quaque sex hora** _____

q.6h. Every 6 hours.

9. **quaque octa hora** _____

q.8h. Every 8 hours.

10. **quater in die** _____

q.i.d. Four times a day.

11. **ter in die** _____

t.i.d. Three times a day.

II. FILL IN THE BLANK.
Expand the following abbreviations. Expand the abbreviated forms to their English equivalent or use the English term for the Latin word.

1. p.m. _____

2. t.i.d. _____

3. pro re nata _____

4. q.i.d. _____

5. q.2h. _____

6. q.d. _____

7. quaque hora _____

8. quaque _____

Unit 5
Word Differentiation

Word Differentiation – Introduction

You may remember from the study of prefixes and suffixes such terms as *inter-/intra-* and *-phasia/-phagia*. Examples of such look-alike/sound-alike words are not uncommon in medical terminology.

This unit focuses on these sound-alike/look-alike words.

Pay careful attention to the spelling, because a single letter can change the entire meaning of the sentence.

Memorize the meanings so that you can consistently identify the meaning of these words in a medical report without having to consult a dictionary every time.

As you work through this unit, look carefully at all the examples given. You will see medical terminology used in context, just as you will see it in the workplace.

We've thrown a few laughs in this unit for you—after all similar sounding words can be fun!

Medical Humor

"The eleventh pun always gets a laugh, even if no pun in ten did." – Anonymous

Word Differentiation – Lesson 1

1. **accept** versus **except**

   accept – To receive willingly; to agree to.
   She accepted the risks and benefits and agreed to proceed with the treatment.

   except – To take out or leave out; not including; other than.
   There were no complications, except for the excessive bleeding.

2. **adenocyst** versus **adenosis**

   adenocyst – An adenoma in which there is cyst formation.
   The biopsy returned a diagnosis of adenocyst.

   adenosis – Any disease of the glands; the abnormal development or formation of gland tissue.
   The physical examination indicated that there was adenosis in the submandibular gland.

3. **affect** versus **effect**

   affect – To produce an effect or change on or to exert an influence over.
   The digitalis did affect his heart condition.

   effect – To cause to come into being, to bring about, accomplish, execute.
   The surgeon's skill was adequate to effect a resolution of the patient's problem.

4. **afferent** versus **efferent**

   afferent – Conveying TOWARD a center.
   There was an afferent loop noted in the colon.

   efferent – Conveying AWAY FROM a center.
   The efferent nerve was followed.

5. **allusion** versus **delusion** versus **elusion** versus **illusion**

   allusion – To refer indirectly or by suggestion.
   He made an allusion to an earlier incident.

   delusion – A false belief that is firmly maintained in spite of proof or evidence to the contrary, as when a patient believes he is Napoleon or Jesus.
   In spite of years of treatment, his delusions of grandeur were out of control.

   elusion – Escaping the notice of, an avoidance of, the eluding of something.
   The escapee was a master of elusion.

   illusion – A mistaken idea; a misleading image presented to the vision.
   The optical illusion of water flowing up the waterfall was enough to nauseate the patient.

I. **MATCHING.**
   Match the correct term to the definition.

   1. ____ afferent
   2. ____ illusion
   3. ____ affect
   4. ____ except
   5. ____ adenocyst
   6. ____ effect
   7. ____ accept
   8. ____ elusion
   9. ____ efferent
   10. ____ adenosis
   11. ____ effective
   12. ____ affective

   A. a misleading image
   B. to agree to
   C. disease of the glands
   D. productive of results
   E. the avoidance of
   F. expression of emotion
   G. to leave out
   H. arising from emotions
   I. away from the center
   J. the result or outcome
   K. toward the center
   L. an adenoma

MULTIPLE CHOICE.
   Select the correct answer.

1. We were unable to help him to (⊙ accept, ⊙ except) his mother's death.

2. He seemed to be deeply (⊙ affected, ⊙ effected) by the loss of his dog.

3. He continued to experience (⊙ allusions, ⊙ elusions, ⊙ delusions) when taking the prescribed medication.

4. We told him to discontinue all medicines (⊙ accept, ⊙ except) for the Haldol.

5. (⊙ Affective, ⊙ Effective) use of drugs requires knowledge of their side effects.

6. As it is experimental, all of the side (⊙ affects, ⊙ effects) are yet unknown.

7. An (⊙ afferent, ⊙ efferent) loop was noted toward the center of the abdomen.

8. He made continued (⊙ allusions, ⊙ elusions, ⊙ illusions) to a traumatic experience while in the war.

9. There was no cyst formation; therefore, (⊙ adenocyst, ⊙ adenosis) was ruled out as possible etiology.

10. There was the inexplicable (⊙ allusion, ⊙ elusion, ⊙ illusion) of the palpated mass on ultrasound.

11. He was diagnosed with a schizo (⊙ affective, ⊙ effective) disorder.

12. There was evidence of (⊙ adenocyst, ⊙ adenosis) in the parotid gland.

Word Differentiation – Lesson 2

1. **aide** versus **aid**

   aide – A person who acts as an assistant, as an aide-de-camp, nurse's aide, or teacher's aide. In Alaskan Eskimo villages, most routine healthcare is provided by village health aides.

   aid – Assistance; an assisting device, as a hearing aid, orthotic aid, or aid in transfers. The orthopedic surgeon prescribed a walker as an aid to ambulation.

2. **access** versus **axis**

   access – Capacity to enter or approach; to get to. She consented to allow access to her files.

   axis – A line about which a revolving body turns or about which a structure would turn if it did revolve; the second cervical vertebra. It was noted to move normally about the axis.

3. **anuresis** versus **enuresis**

    anuresis – Retention of urine in the bladder.
    A Foley catheter was placed secondary to his anuresis.

    enuresis – The involuntary discharge of urine after the age at which urinary control should have been achieved.
    The mother brought the child back for continued enuresis.

4. **acidic** versus **ascitic**

    acidic – Of or pertaining to an acid; acid-forming.
    The urine had an acidic quality to it.

    ascitic – Pertaining to or characterized by ascites: the effusion and accumulation of serous fluid in the abdominal cavity.
    The abdominal cavity was filled with ascitic fluid.

5. **arthrectomy** versus **atherectomy**

    arthrectomy – The excision of a joint.
    He had arthrectomy of his metatarsophalangeal joint.

    atherectomy – The excision of an atheromatous plaque (from an artery).
    There was atherectomy performed of the affected artery.

6. **atonic** versus **atopic** versus **atoxic** versus **atrophic** versus **ectopic**

    atonic – Lacking normal tone or strength.
    Her uterus was markedly atonic.

    atopic – Pertaining to atopy (a genetic predisposition toward the development of hypersensitivity reactions against common environmental antigens = allergies).
    The patient has been applying Cortizone—10 Maximum Strength to his atopic dermatitis.

    atoxic – Not poisonous; not due to a poison.
    The fluids in his stomach were found to be atoxic.

    atrophic – Pertaining to or characterized by atrophy (wasting away; a diminution in the size of a cell, tissue, organ, or part).
    His muscles were atrophic secondary to his extended hospitalization.

    ectopic – Pertaining to or characterized by displacement or malposition; located away from normal position; arising from abnormal site or tissue.
    She was noted on ultrasound to have a positive ectopic pregnancy.

I. MATCHING.
Match the correct term to the definition.

1. ____ ascitic
2. ____ enuresis
3. ____ axis
4. ____ atherectomy
5. ____ atrophic
6. ____ atoxic
7. ____ acidic
8. ____ ectopic
9. ____ aid
10. ____ anuresis
11. ____ atopic
12. ____ atonic
13. ____ aide
14. ____ access

A. line revolved about
B. acid-forming
C. displaced
D. wasting away
E. retention of urine
F. excision of arterial plaque
G. to get at
H. serous fluid in the abdomen
I. involuntary discharge of urine
J. not poisonous
K. lacking strength
L. pertaining to allergies
M. assisting device
N. person who assists

II. MULTIPLE CHOICE.
Choose the best answer.

1. There was marked (○ acidic, ○ ascitic) fluid forming in the abdomen.

2. There was (○ arthrectomy, ○ atherectomy) performed of the interphalangeal joint.

3. We worked for three months trying to resolve the child's (○ anuresis, ○ enuresis).

4. She was admitted emergently to undergo removal of her (○ atopic, ○ atrophic, ○ atoxic, ○ ectopic) pregnancy.

5. There was an (○ acidic, ○ ascitic) component to the aspirated fluid.

6. She required placement of a Foley catheter secondary to (○ anuresis, ○ enuresis).

7. As part of the heart procedure, an (○ arthrectomy, ○ atherectomy) was performed of the Left Intermediate Mammary Artery.

8. There was (○ atony, ○ atopy, ○ atrophy) of the extremities following the seizure.

9. We were unable to gain (○ access, ○ axis) to the mass forming in her abdomen.

10. The drug was determined to be ($\bigcirc$ atopic, $\bigcirc$ atonic, $\bigcirc$ atoxic, $\bigcirc$ atrophic).

11. The patient received ($\bigcirc$ aide, $\bigcirc$ aid) at home by a home nursing aide.

Word Differentiation – Lesson 3

1. **aural** versus **oral**

   aural – Pertaining to or perceived by the ear.
   He responded with severe pain to aural stimulus.

   oral – Pertaining to the mouth; taken through or applied in the mouth.
   There were no oral lesions.

2. **bolus** versus **bullous**

   bolus – A rounded mass of food or medicinal preparation ready to swallow, or such a mass passing through the gastrointestinal tract; a mass of pharmaceutical preparation given intravenously for diagnostic purposes.
   She was given a bolus of Pitocin immediately following delivery.

   bullous – Pertaining to or characterized by bullae (a large vesicle, more than 5 mm in circumference, containing serous or seropurulent fluid; also called a bleb or a blister).
   There was bullous disease in the lungs.

3. **brachial** versus **branchial** versus **bronchial**

   brachial – Pertaining to the arm.
   There was brachial swelling noted.

   branchial – Pertaining to or resembling the gills of a fish and having reference to structures in the lateral neck.
   She has a branchial cleft cyst.

   bronchial – Pertaining to one or more bronchi (a subdivision of any of the larger air passages of the lungs).
   There was bronchial wall thickening.

4. **bulbus** versus **bulbous**

   bulbus – A rounded mass or enlargement.
   The aortic bulbus was normal.

   bulbous – Having the form or nature of a bulb; bearing or arising from a bulb.
   There was swelling on the bulbous urethra.

5. **callus** versus **callous**

   callus – Localized hyperplasia of the horny layer of the epidermis due to pressure or friction. (noun or verb)
   The x-ray showed a callus on the fracture.

   callous – Hard, callus-like. (adj or verb)
   There was a callous lesion on the surface of the foot.

I. MATCHING.
Match the correct term to the definition.

1. ____ brachial
2. ____ bulbous
3. ____ aural
4. ____ bronchial
5. ____ bolus
6. ____ callus
7. ____ oral
8. ____ bullous
9. ____ branchial
10. ____ bulbus
11. ____ callous

A. pertaining to the ear
B. pertaining to the arm
C. medicinal mass
D. hard
E. rounded enlargement
F. characterized by bullae
G. resembling fish gills
H. air passage in the lungs
I. pertaining to the mouth
J. localized hyperplasia of the epidermis
K. bulb-like

II. MULTIPLE CHOICE.
Select the best answer.

1. She was given a large (◯ bolus, ◯ bullous) of the medication.

2. A diagnosis of (◯ brachial, ◯ branchial, ◯ bronchial) cleft cyst was made.

3. On (◯ aural, ◯ oral) examination, her tongue was noted to be midline.

4. The anterior urethra consists of the (◯ bulbous, ◯ bulbus) urethra, the pendulous urethra, and the glandular urethra.

5. Extremities examination revealed marked (◯ brachial, ◯ branchial, ◯ bronchial) swelling.

6. Tympanic membranes are red and bulging on (◯ aural, ◯ oral) examination.

7. On x-ray a (◯ callous, ◯ callus) was noted, which indicated healing of the fracture.

8. The lung fields showed marked (◯ bolus, ◯ bullous) changes.

9. The ocular (◯ bulbous, ◯ bulbus) is often referred to as the eye.

10. The patient was given a diagnosis of (◯ brachial, ◯ branchial, ◯ bronchial) pneumonia.

Word Differentiation – Lesson 4

1. **canalization** versus **cannulization**

   canalization – The natural formation of canals within a structure or the surgical creation of canals for drainage.
   There was canalization noted throughout the abdominal cavity.

   cannulization – The surgical insertion of a cannula (a tube). (The preferred word is cannulation, but cannulization is used and acceptable.)
   He underwent cannulization in preparation for the operative procedure.

2. **carotid** versus **parotid**

   carotid – Relating to the principal artery of the neck.
   The carotid artery showed normal pulse and sensation.

   parotid – Situated or occurring near the ear, most commonly as in the parotid gland.
   The parotid gland was normal.

3. **claustrum** versus **colostrum**

   claustrum – The thin layer of gray matter lateral to the external capsule of the lentiform nucleus, separating the nucleus from the white substance of the insula.
   The claustrum was intact.

   colostrum – The thin, yellow, milky fluid secreted by the mammary gland shortly before and a few days after delivery of an infant.
   The baby was receiving colostrum upon breastfeeding.

4. **coaptation** versus **coarctation**

   coaptation – Approximation, as in the edges of a wound or fracture.
   Coaptation of the wound edges was carried out.

   coarctation – A condition of stricture or contraction.
   Coarctation of the aorta was noted.

5. **coarse** versus **course**

   coarse – Not fine, rough/harsh.
   There were coarse crackles noted throughout the lung bases.

   course – Direction of progress; sequence of events; a series of instruction periods; the ground or path over which something moves.
   Her postoperative course was without complications.

I. MATCHING.
Match the correct term to the definition.

1. ___ canalization

2. ___ claustrum

3. ___ course

4. ___ coarctation

5. ___ colostrums

6. ___ coarse

7. ___ cannulization

8. ___ parotid

9. ___ coaptation

10. ___ carotid

A. neck artery
B. approximation
C. milky fluid
D. rough or harsh
E. near the ear
F. cannula insertion
G. contraction
H. direction of progress
I. layer of grey matter
J. canal formation

II. MULTIPLE CHOICE.
Select the best answer.

1. His voice had a (◯ coarse, ◯ course) quality to it.

2. There was (◯ canalization, ◯ cannulization) noted in the patient's pelvic cavity.

3. The (◯ carotid, ◯ parotid) gland was noted to be swollen.

4. On examination of the brain, the (◯ claustrum, ◯ colostrum) was within normal limits.

5. (◯ Carotid, ◯ Parotid) pulses were intact.

6. Upon successful placement of the drainage tube, (◯ canalization, ◯ cannulization) was achieved.

7. Throughout the (◯ coarse, ◯ course) of hospitalization, her delusional thinking improved.

8. We proceeded with (◯ coaptation, ◯ coarctation) of the wound edges.

9. The baby was having trouble extracting the (◯ claustrum, ◯ colostrum).

10. There was marked (◯ coaptation, ◯ coarctation) of the esophagus.

Word Differentiation – Lesson 5

1. **complement** versus **compliment**

    complement – A quantity needed to make a thing complete; to be complementary to (supplying a defect, making complete, accessory).
    He was given Ensure to complement his diet.

    compliment – An expression of courtesy; a flattering remark OR to pay a compliment.
    I complimented him on his choice of words.

2. **conscience** versus **conscious**

    conscience – Aware of the moral right and wrong of one's actions.
    He had an extremely guilty conscience.

    conscious – Aware; mentally awake or alert.
    He was not conscious when he was found.

3. **COR/cor** versus **core** versus **corps**

    COR/cor – The muscular organ that maintains the circulation of the blood (the heart). If a patient requests that no heroic measures, such as tubes, cardiopulmonary resuscitation, respirators, etc. be used to prolong his life, he is placed on what is called NO COR status. This is ALWAYS typed in ALL CAPS.
    He was given a diagnosis of cor pulmonale.

    core – The central part of anything.
    A core of tissue was obtained.

    corps – An organized subdivision of a country's military forces.
    She joined the corps.
    He is on active duty with the Marine Corps.

4. **coracoid** versus **choroid**

    coracoid – Like a raven's beak (the coracoid process of the scapula).
    There was a small spur noted off the coracoid process.

    choroid – The thin, pigmented, vascular coat of the eye, furnishing blood to the retina and conducting arteries and nerves to the anterior structures.
    The choroid plexus is intact.

5. **cytology** versus **sitology**

    cytology – The study of cells (their origin, structure, function, and pathology).
    Her cytology exam came back negative.

    sitology – The sum of knowledge regarding food, diet, and nutrition.
    The patient's recent sitology is uncertain, as the patient is a poor historian.

I. MATCHING.
Match the correct term to the definition.

1. ____ coracoid
2. ____ COR
3. ____ cytology
4. ____ compliment
5. ____ core
6. ____ conscience
7. ____ choroids
8. ____ complement
9. ____ conscious
10. ____ corps
11. ____ sitology

A. flattering remark
B. beak-shaped
C. military division
D. coating of the eye
E. awake and alert
F. accessory
G. knowledge of nutrition
H. center
I. the heart
J. moral indicator
K. study of cells

II. MULTIPLE CHOICE.
Select the best answer.

1. He worked for the (◯ Cor, ◯ Core, ◯ Corps) of Engineers.

2. He was given (◯ complementary, ◯ complimentary) antibiotic supplementation.

3. The (◯ coracoid, ◯ choroid) process was intact.

4. He was (◯ conscience, ◯ conscious) on presentation to the emergency room.

5. (◯ Cytology, ◯ Sitology) brought back a diagnosis of squamous cell carcinoma.

6. She received (◯ complements, ◯ compliments) from the nursing staff on her progress.

7. Biopsy yielded a (◯ COR, ◯ core, ◯ corps) of negative tissue.

8. On retinal examination the (◯ coracoid, ◯ choroid) plexus was normal.

9. Her status was NO (◯ COR, ◯ CORE, ◯ CORPS).

10. His delusional behavior appears to be the result of nothing more than a guilty (◯ conscience, ◯ conscious).

Word Differentiation – Lesson 6

1. **die** versus **dye**

   die – To stop living.
   He kept saying that he wanted to die.

   dye – Material used for coloring and staining as tests and as therapeutic agents in medicine.
   Dye was injected after the procedure was begun.

2. **discreet** versus **discrete**

   discreet – Showing good judgment; capable of observing prudent silence.
   He was discreet approaching the subject.

   discrete – Individually distinct, noncontinuous.
   There were no discrete calcifications.

3. **dysphagia** versus **dysphasia** versus **dysplasia**

   dysphagia – Difficulty swallowing.
   He came in complaining of severe dysphagia.

   dysphasia – Impairment of speech.
   She had dysphasia secondary to a cerebrovascular accident two years ago.

   dysplasia – Abnormality of development; in pathology, alteration in size, shape, and organization of adult cells.
   Dysplasia was noted on biopsy.

4. **echos** versus **echoes**

   echos – The plural form of the shortened word echocardiogram.
   His echos all showed T-wave depression.

   echoes – The plural form of the word echorepetition of a sound or the reflection of ultrasonic, radio, and radar waves.
   Cardiac echoes were heard.

5. **elicit** versus **illicit**

   elicit – To draw out or forth.
   We could not elicit any further information.

   illicit – Not permitted, unlawful.
   He does not take any illicit drugs.

I. MATCHING.
Match the correct term to the definition.

1. ___ dye
2. ___ elicit
3. ___ dysplasia
4. ___ illicit
5. ___ echoes
6. ___ die
7. ___ dysphasia
8. ___ discreet
9. ___ dysphagia
10. ___ echos
11. ___ discrete

A. difficulty swallowing
B. to stop living
C. plural echocardiogram
D. individually distinct
E. impairment of speech
F. to draw out
G. illegal
H. abnormal development
I. material for coloring
J. repetition of sound
K. showing good judgment

II. MULTIPLE CHOICE.
Select the best answer.

1. There were no (○ discreet, ○ discrete) calcifications.

2. We tried to (○ elicit, ○ illicit) information from her.

3. Following injection of the contrast (○ die, ○ dye) we performed the procedure.

4. The patient had complaints of (○ dysphagia, ○ dysphasia, ○ dysplasia) with all kinds of food.

5. Her (○ echos, ○ echoes) were all within normal limits.

6. She drinks a moderate amount of alcohol and is on no (○ elicit, ○ illicit) drugs.

7. The patient expressed a wish to (○ die, ○ dye).

8. The patient suffered from (○ dysphagia, ○ dysphasia, ○ dysplasia) secondary to her stroke.

9. There were increased (○ echos, ○ echoes) on the examination.

10. When talking about his family life, he was generally very (◯ discreet, ◯ discrete).

11. There was marked (◯ dysphagia, ◯ dysphasia, ◯ dysplasia) on pathological examination.

Word Differentiation – Lesson 7

1. **enervation** versus **innervation**

   enervation – Lack of nervous energy; removal of a nerve or a section of a nerve.
   Subsequently he underwent enervation.

   innervation – The distribution or supply of nerves to a part; the supply of nervous energy or of nerve stimulus sent to a part.
   The innervation to the hand was within normal limits.

2. **enterocleisis** versus **enteroclysis**

   enterocleisis – Closure of a wound in the intestine; occlusion of the lumen of the intestine.
   Following thorough inspection, he underwent enterocleisis of the small intestine.

   enteroclysis – The injection of a nutrient or medicinal liquid into the bowel; the introduction of barium directly into the small bowel through a nasogastric tube.
   Following insertion of an NG tube, enteroclysis was undertaken.

3. **exacerbation** versus **exasperation**

   exacerbation – Increase in the severity of a disease or any of its symptoms.
   He had exacerbation of appendicitis symptoms.

   exasperation – Being vexed or irritated.
   She experienced exasperation with the hospital staff.

4. **exenterate** versus **exonerate**

   exenterate – To remove the contents of a part of the body, especially the orbit of the eye or the paranasal sinuses.
   He underwent exenteration of the paranasal sinuses in an effort to solve the problem of chronic sinusitis with postnasal drainage.

   exonerate – To free from blame or reproach.
   He was exonerated from all criminal charges.

5. **eyelet** versus **islet**

   eyelet – A small, round, usually reinforced hole in leather, cloth, or sailcloth, for a lace, ring, or rope to pass through; fabric having cut-out designs with embroidered edges.
   She was wearing a pretty white eyelet pinafore.

   islet – Islands or islets of Langerhans, clusters of cells within the pancreas that produce secretions such as insulin. These are composed of islet cells, and malignancies related to them are islet cell tumors, such as insuloma, gastrinoma, glucagonoma, and somatostatinoma.
   The islets of Langerhans are part of the endocrine system.

6. **facial** versus **fascial**

> **facial** – Of or pertaining to the face.
> On HEENT examination there was severe facial swelling.

> **fascial** – Pertaining to or of the nature of a fascia (a sheet or band of fibrous tissue such as lies deep to the skin or forms an investment for muscles and various other organs of the body).
> The cellulitis extended into the fascial layer.

7. **facies** versus **feces**

> **facies** – A term used in anatomical designation of a) the anterior or ventral aspect of the head, forehead to chin inclusive and b) a specific surface of a body structure, part, or organ; the expression or appearance of the face.
> The facies demonstrated fetal alcohol syndrome features.

> **feces** – The excrement discharged from the intestines.
> There is feces scattered throughout the colon.

I. **MATCHING.**
Match the correct term to the definition.

1. ___ exacerbation		A.	pertaining to the face
2. ___ enterocleisis		B.	being irritated
3. ___ enervation		C.	removal of a nerve
4. ___ innervation		D.	closure of a wound
5. ___ feces		E.	barium injection
6. ___ exasperation		F.	excrement
7. ___ fascial		G.	fibrous tissue
8. ___ enteroclysis		H.	increase of symptoms
9. ___ facies		I.	expression of face
10. ___ facial		J.	nerve distribution

II. **MULTIPLE CHOICE.**
Select the best answer.

1. The colon was packed with (◯ facies, ◯ feces).

2. Following (◯ enervation, ◯ innervation) the wound was closed.

3. The incision was taken down through the (◯ facial, ◯ fascial) plane.

4. The patient experienced an acute (◯ exacerbation, ◯ exasperation) of abdominal pain.

5. Following abdominal exploration, the patient underwent (◯ enterocleisis, ◯ enteroclysis).

6. (◯ Enervation, ◯ Innervation) of the foot was within normal limits.

7. The patient has normal (◯ facies, ◯ feces).

8. Following informed written consent, (◯ enterocleisis, ◯ enteroclysis) was started.

9. The patient had feelings of (◯ exacerbation, ◯ exasperation) regarding her progress.

10. The patient experienced a blow to the eye and had severe (◯ facial, ◯ fascial) swelling.

Review: Lessons 1-7

I. MATCHING.
Match the correct term to the definition.

1. ___ adenocyst	A.	of or pertaining to an acid; acid-forming
2. ___ adenosis	B.	any disease of the glands; abnormal development or formation of gland tissue
3. ___ acidic	C.	aware; mentally awake or alert
4. ___ ascitic	D.	an adenoma in which there is cyst formation
5. ___ carotid	E.	aware of the moral right and wrong of one's actions
	F.	relating to the principal artery of the neck
6. ___ parotid	G.	pertaining to or characterized by ascites: the effusion and accumulation of serous fluid in the abdominal cavity
7. ___ conscience		
8. ___ conscious	H.	situated or occuring near the ear, most commonly as in the parotid gland

II. FILL IN THE BLANK.
Enter the correct word in the blank provided.

1. Showing good judgment; capable of observing prudent silence.

   _____

2. Plural form of the word echo—repetition of a sound or the reflection of ultrasonic, radio, and radar waves.

   _____

3. Also called islands, clusters of cells within the pancreas that produce secretions such as insulin. _____

4. Individually distinct, noncontinuous. _____

5. Small, round hole in leather, cloth or sailcloth for a lace, ring or rope to pass through. _____

6. Plural form of the shortened word echocardiogram.

   _____

| echoes |
| echos |
| islet |
| eyelet |
| discreet |
| discrete |

Word Differentiation – Lesson 8

1. **fecal** versus **cecal** versus **thecal**

   fecal – Pertaining to or of the nature of feces.
   The patient had a large amount of fecal material scattered throughout the colon.

   cecal – Pertaining to the cecum (any blind pouch or cul-de-sac, usually the first part of the large intestine).
   He underwent ileocecal pouch anastomosis.

   thecal – Pertaining to the theca (an enclosing case or sheath— usually referring to the sac of the spine).
   The mass extended up to the thecal sac.

2. **flexor** versus **flexure**

   flexor – Any muscle that flexes a joint.
   On arthroscopy the flexor tendon was intact.

   flexure – A bending; a bent portion of a structure or organ.
   On colonoscopy exam the hepatic flexure was normal.

3. **fundal** versus **fungal**

   fundal – Pertaining to a fundus (the bottom or base of anything, usually the base of an organ).
   The mass was located fundal to the liver.

   fungal – Pertaining to or caused by fungus.
   He had a fungal infection.

4. **homogeneous** versus **homogenous**

> **homogeneous** – Consisting of or composed of similar elements or ingredients; of a uniform quality throughout.
> There was homogeneous echotexture throughout the kidney.
>
> **homogenous** – Having a similarity of structure because of descent from a common ancestor.
> The population of Finland is quite homogenous, while the population of the U.S. is not.

5. **hyalin** versus **hyaline**

> **hyalin** – A translucent albuminoid substance, one of the products of amyloid degeneration; a substance composing the walls of hydatid cysts.
> The cyst wall was composed of hyalin material.
>
> **hyaline** – Glassy and transparent, or nearly so.
> The baby was diagnosed with hyaline membrane disease.

I. MATCHING.
Match the correct term to the definition.

1. ___ fecal		A. glassy or transparent
2. ___ fundal		B. sharing an ancestor
		C. pertaining to the cecum
3. ___ hyalin		D. at the bottom
4. ___ thecal		E. a muscle flexing a joint
5. ___ homogeneous		F. pertaining to excrement
		G. caused by a fungus
6. ___ flexure		H. albuminoid substance
7. ___ homogenous		I. sac in the spine
8. ___ flexor		J. a bending
		K. uniform quality
9. ___ cecal		
10. ___ hyaline		
11. ___ fungal		

II. MULTIPLE CHOICE.
Select the best answer.

1. The cyst was in a (◯ fundal, ◯ fungal) location.

2. There was a (◯ homogeneous, ◯ homogenous) component to the virus.

3. The hepatic (◯ flexor, ◯ flexure) was noted to be normal.

4. There was a (◯ fecal, ◯ cecal, ◯ thecal) residual in the colon.

5. Changes on x-ray examination are probably due to (◯ hyalin, ◯ hyaline) membrane disease.

6. Spine x-ray showed a normal (◯ fecal, ◯ cecal, ◯ thecal) sac.

7. (◯ Flexor, ◯ Flexure) tendon functioned normally.

8. There was (◯ homogeneous, ◯ homogenous) echotexture of the liver.

9. The ileo-(◯ fecal, ◯ cecal, ◯ thecal) valve was seen and was normal.

10. He was given medications for presumed (◯ fundal, ◯ fungal) infection.

Medical Humor

A few books for your word collection:

How To Predict the Future by Horace Cope
The Tiger's Revenge by Claude Butz
Modern Accounting by Cook, Books, and Hyde
How I Got My Start in Life by Robin Banks

Word Differentiation – Lesson 9

1. **ileum** versus **ilium**

   ileum – The distal portion of the small intestine, extending from the jejunum to the cecum.
   The terminal ileum was identified.

   ilium – The expansive superior portion of the hip bone.
   The ilium showed healing, as evidenced by callus formation.

2. **induction** versus **introduction**

   induction – The act or process of inducing or causing to occur—especially the production of anesthesia or unconsciousness by use of the appropriate agents.
   The patient underwent Pitocin induction of labor.

   introduction – Leading or bringing in, especially for the first time; to put in.
   Introduction of the Cordis catheter was via the left subclavian approach.

3. **install** versus **instill**

   install – (installation) To establish in an indicated place, condition, or status; to set up for use or service.
   We installed a video camera in the observation room.

   instill – (instillation) To cause to enter drop by drop; to impart gradually.
   Following instillation of a morphine drip, he was taken off p.o. medications.

4. **intralocular** versus **intraocular**

> **intralocular** – Within the loculi (small space or cavity) of a structure.
> He had intralocular calcifications within the lungs.
>
> **intraocular** – Within the eye.
> The patient underwent intraocular lens implantation.

5. **malleolus** versus **malleus**

> **malleolus** – A rounded process, usually the protuberance on either side of the ankle joint.
> The medial malleolus was intact.
>
> **malleus** – The largest of the auditory ossicles, and the one attached to the membrana tympani.
> The cochlea and malleus were entirely normal.

I. **MATCHING.**
    Match the correct term to the definition.

1. ___ instill		A. auditory ossicle
2. ___ introduction		B. hip bone
		C. within the eye
3. ___ malleolus		D. portion of small intestine
4. ___ install		E. rounded process
5. ___ intralocular		F. establishing anesthesia
		G. to establish in place
6. ___ ilium		H. within a cavity
7. ___ malleus		I. enter drop by drop
8. ___ induction		J. leading or bringing in
9. ___ ileum		
10. ___ intraocular		

II. **MULTIPLE CHOICE.**
     Select the best answer.

1. Following (◯ installation, ◯ instillation) of contrast, the upper GI examination was done.

2. The lateral (◯ malleolus, ◯ malleus) was inspected and found to be entirely within normal limits.

3. The (◯ ileum, ◯ ilium) was not able to be visualized on the film of the pelvis.

4. She underwent (◯ induction, ◯ introduction) of general anesthesia.

5. The (◯ malleolus, ◯ malleus) and vestibula were normal.

6. The ($\bigcirc$ ileo-, $\bigcirc$ ilio-) cecal valve is normal.

7. The new beds will be ($\bigcirc$ installed, $\bigcirc$ instilled) in the rooms in one week.

8. There were bullous changes in the ($\bigcirc$ intralocular, $\bigcirc$ intraocular) areas of the lungs.

9. We will recheck his values following ($\bigcirc$ induction, $\bigcirc$ introduction) of his new regimen of medicines.

10. The ($\bigcirc$ intralocular, $\bigcirc$ intraocular) lens was implanted.

Word Differentiation – Lesson 10

1. **median sternotomy** versus **mediastinotomy**

   median sternotomy – The operation of cutting through the midline of the sternum.
   He underwent median sternotomy to begin his heart surgery.

   mediastinotomy – The operation of cutting into the mediastinum (the mass of tissues and organs separating the two pleural sacs).
   X-ray showed evidence of recent mediastinotomy.

2. **mental** versus **omental**

   mental – Pertaining to the mind or chin (mentum).
   Mental status is slightly delusional.

   omental – Pertaining to the omentum (a fold of peritoneum extending from the stomach to adjacent organ in the abdominal cavity).
   There was omental obscuration on the abdominal film secondary to poor technique.

3. **metaphysis** versus **metastasis**

   metaphysis – The wider part of the extremity of the shaft of a long bone, adjacent to the epiphyseal disk.
   There was evidence of widening of the metaphysis of the humerus.

   metastasis – The transfer of disease from one organ or part to another not directly connected with it (usually referring to malignancy).
   On bone scan there was evidence of metastasis to the lower spine.

4. **mucous*** versus **mucus***

   mucous* – Pertaining to or resembling mucus; adjectival form of mucus.
   The mucous membranes are normal.

   mucus* – The free slime of the mucous membranes, composed of secretion of the glands, etc.
   On sinus examination there was a great deal of mucus.

5. **osteal** versus **ostial**

   osteal – Bony, osseous.
   He had congenital osteal deformities.

ostial – Pertaining to an ostium (a door or opening; used to designate an opening into a tubular organ or between two distinct cavities).
There was ostial thickening noted.

The difference between these two terms is that the -ous ending is an adjectival ending and is used in describing another word (such as membrane). This rule is appropriate for other medical terms, such as viscus/viscous, callus/callous, or bulbus/bulbous, the only difference being the adjectival use.

I. MATCHING.
Match the correct term to the definition.

1. ____ ostial		A. mediastinal operation
2. ____ mucus		B. pertaining to the mind
		C. a fold of the peritoneum (adj)
3. ____ metastasis		D. part of the long bone
4. ____ osteal		E. cutting through the sternum
		F. spread of disease
5. ____ mucous		G. resembling mucus
6. ____ mediastinotomy		H. bony, osseous
7. ____ metaphysis		I. free slime
		J. pertaining to a door
8. ____ median sternotomy		
9. ____ mental		
10. ____ omental		

II. MULTIPLE CHOICE.
Select the best answer.

1. The bony (◯ metaphysis, ◯ metastasis) of the femur was calcified.

2. There was a buildup of (◯ mucous, ◯ mucus) behind the ethmoid sinus.

3. There was (◯ osteal, ◯ ostial) thickening of the aorta.

4. A (◯ median sternotomy, ◯ mediastinotomy) was performed prior to the coronary artery bypass grafting.

5. The (◯ mucous, ◯ mucus) membranes appeared normal.

6. On (◯ mental, ◯ omental) status examination there was clarity of thought.

7. The patient's x-ray revealed marked (◯ metaphysis, ◯ metastasis) to all major organs.

8. The patient had (◯ osteal, ◯ ostial) pain in her ankles.

9. A (◯ median sternotomy, ◯ mediastinotomy) was performed secondary to metastasis to the mediastinum.

10. The (◯ mental, ◯ omentum) was noted to be intact.

Word Differentiation – Lesson 11

1. **parental** versus **parenteral**

   parental – Pertaining to one that begets offspring.
   Following informed parental consent, the ORIF was performed on the child.

   parenteral – Not through the alimentary canal, but rather by injection through some other route, such as subcutaneous, intramuscular, intravenous, etc.
   The patient was begun on total parenteral nutrition.

2. **perineal** versus **peroneal** versus **perennial** versus **perianal** versus **peritoneal**

   perineal – Pertaining to the part of the body situated behind the pubic arch, in front of the coccyx, between the upper thighs—in other words, the crotch.
   Her gynecological symptoms included severe perineal itching.

   peroneal – Pertaining to the outer part of the leg, over the fibula and peroneal nerve.
   Peroneal muscle atrophy is a predominantly inherited disease that is characterized by weakening of the foot and ankle muscles.

   perennial – In horticulture, a plant that remains alive through a number of years; generally, something that lasts through a long, indefinite, or infinite time.
   She seemed to be perennially ill, although the doctors could never really determine what her specific problems were.

   perianal – Referring to the area around the anus.
   She had a history of recurrent perianal abscess.

   peritoneal – Pertaining to the serous membrane lining the abdominopelvic walls. When this word is spoken rapidly, it is difficult or impossible to hear the "t."
   Incision was made through the peritoneal membrane.

3. **perineum** versus **peritoneum**

   perineum – The region between the thighs.
   On digital examination the perineum was found to be normal.

   peritoneum – The serous membrane lining the abdominopelvic walls.
   On exploration of the abdomen, the peritoneum was noted to be intact.

4. **plain** versus **plane**

> **plain** – Free of extraneous matter; simple, uncomplicated; lacking beauty.
> On plain film examination of the abdomen there was a mass noted behind the liver.

> **plane** – A surface such that a straight line connecting any two of its points lies wholly in the surface.
> Films were taken in the sagittal plane.

5. **precede** versus **proceed**

> **precede** – To be, go, or come ahead or in front of.
> Preceding the instillation of general anesthesia, the patient's vital signs were recorded.

> **proceed** – To go on in an orderly way; continue.
> We proceeded to carry the incision down through the subcutaneous layer.

I. MATCHING.
Match the correct term to the definition.

1. ____ plain	A.	area between the thighs
2. ____ proceed	B.	pertaining to parents
3. ____ peritoneum	C.	to go in front of
4. ____ peroneal	D.	simple
5. ____ precede	E.	injection by alternate route
6. ____ perineum	F.	pertaining to the perineum
7. ____ plane	G.	continue
8. ____ parenteral	H.	fibular
9. ____ perineal	I.	serous membrane or abdomen
10. ____ parental	J.	a straight surface

II. MULTIPLE CHOICE.
Select the best answer.

1. The (◯ perineum, ◯ peritoneum) was well-visualized on abdominal exam.

2. We decided to (◯ precede, ◯ proceed) with his physical therapy.

3. The (◯ perineal, ◯ peroneal) ligament was torn.

4. We followed the normal (◯ plain, ◯ plane) of dissection.

5. He was begun on total (◯ parental, ◯ parenteral) nutrition.

6. A ($\bigcirc$ plain, $\bigcirc$ plane) film was taken of the head.

7. Consent ($\bigcirc$ preceded, $\bigcirc$ proceeded) hospitalization.

8. The youth is strongly in need of (($\bigcirc$ parental, $\bigcirc$ parenteral) guidance.

9. Her ($\bigcirc$ perineum, $\bigcirc$ peroneum) was torn during intercourse.

Word Differentiation – Lesson 12

1. **perfusion** versus **profusion** versus **protrusion**

   perfusion – The act of pouring over or through, especially the passage of fluid through the vessels of a specific organ.
   There was normal perfusion of the lungs.

   profusion – Abundance, pouring forth with great liberality.
   There was a profusion of mucous discharge from her nose.

   protrusion – The state of being thrust forward.
   There was protrusion of the orthopedic nail through the skin.

2. **prostate** versus **prostrate**

   prostate – A gland in the male that surrounds the neck of the bladder and the urethra.
   Genitourinary exam revealed a normal sized prostate.

   prostrate – Extended in a horizontal position.
   The patient was prostrate upon the ground when the ambulance arrived.

3. **prostatic** versus **prosthetic**

   prostatic – Related to the prostate.
   His benign prostatic hypertrophy exhibited the usual symptoms.

   prosthetic – Referring to an artificial limb or other artificial structure in the body.
   He had a prosthetic heart valve.

4. **reflex** versus **reflux**

   reflex – A reflected action or movement; the sum total of any particular involuntary activity.
   Deep tendon reflexes were 2+ and normal.

   reflux – A backward or return flow.
   The patient presented for symptoms of reflux esophagitis.

5. **regimen** versus **regiment**

   regimen – A strictly regulated scheme of diet, exercise, or other activity designed to achieve certain ends.
   His regimen consisted of Zantac and Diabinese.

   regiment – A military unit.
   His regiment was stationed in Saigon.

6. **residence** versus **residents** versus **resonance**

   residence – The place where one lives.
   His place of residence is 1200 E. University Ave, Nowhere, Maine.

   residents – Those who live in a place; physicians serving in residency.
   The examination was performed by the residents on call.

   resonance – The prolongation and intensification of sound produced by the transmission of its vibrations to a cavity; a vocal sound as heard in auscultation.
   The lungs were normal on resonance exam.

I. MATCHING.
Match the correct term to the definition.

1. ___ prostate	A.	relating to a male gland
2. ___ profusion	B.	male gland
3. ___ resonance	C.	involuntary action
4. ___ perfusion	D.	lying horizontal
5. ___ regimen	E.	abundance
6. ___ reflex	F.	military unit
7. ___ residence	G.	artificial part
8. ___ reflux	H.	where one lives
9. ___ prostrate	I.	pouring over or through
10. ___ regiment	J.	backward flow
11. ___ protrusion	K.	strictly regulated activity
12. ___ prosthetic	L.	being thrust forward
13. ___ prostatic	M.	vocal sound

II. MULTIPLE CHOICE.
Select the best answer.

1. On (◯ perfusion, ◯ profusion, ◯ protrusion) of the lungs, they were entirely normal.

2. A strict (◯ regimen, ◯ regiment) of antibiotics was started.

3. The patient was found on biopsy to have (◯ prostate, ◯ prostrate) cancer.

4. There were normal (◯ reflexes, ◯ refluxes) exhibited throughout the extremities.

5. There was (◯ perfusion, ◯ profusion, ◯ protrusion) of the intestine through the abdominal wall.

6. The patient should remain (◯ prostate, ◯ prostrate) for at least two weeks.

7. There were three (◯ residence, ◯ residents, ◯ resonance) assigned to his care.

8. The PSA was negative for any recurrent (◯ prostatic, ◯ prosthetic) disease.

9. There was a normal (◯ residence, ◯ residents, ◯ resonance) of sound.

10. He was checked for sandfly disease secondary to his (◯ regimen, ◯ regiment) being assigned to the Persian Gulf.

11. The patient was fitted with a (◯ prostatic, ◯ prosthetic) device.

12. The patient had symptoms of (◯ reflex, ◯ reflux) esophagitis.

Medical Humor: Natural Medicine

An anthropologist is studying a primitive society in the middle of the jungle when he develops constipation. Finding he has run out of medicine for that particular type of dysfunction, he tells the medicine doctor of the tribe he is studying. The medicine man tells him not to worry; his people sometimes suffer from the same malady but they simply chew the leaves of a particular fern. The anthropologist, figuring that he has nothing to lose (the fern wasn't poisonous), decided to try this herbal medicine.

The next morning he bumps into the medicine man, who asks if everything came out all right. The anthropologist replied that ferns had, indeed, worked very well, adding, "With fronds like these, who needs enemas?"

Word Differentiation – Lesson 13

1. **root** versus **route**

   root – The lowermost part, or a structure by which something is firmly attached.
   The aortic root was identified and appeared normal.

   route – Channel; a line of travel.
   The catheter was passed through the internal jugular route.

2. **Scarpa's** versus **scarpus**

   Scarpa's – The deep membranous layer of subcutaneous abdominal fascia.
   An incision was made lateral to Scarpa's fascia.

   scarpus – Not a real word.

3. **shoddy** versus **shotty**

   shoddy – Of poor quality. Not likely to appear very often in a medical context.
   The workmanship on the expensive clothing she bought was really quite shoddy.

   shotty – On palpation, having a texture like buckshot or BBs.
   There were shotty lymph nodes in the axillae.

4. **silicon** versus **silicone**

   silicon – A nonmetallic element occurring in nature.
   There was a heavy concentration of silicon in the dirt.

   silicone – Any organic compound in which all or part of the carbon has been replaced by silicon.
   The patient has had a previous silicone breast implant.

5. **sight** versus **site**

   sight – The process, function, or power of seeing.
   The patient has very poor sight in his left eye.

   site – A place, position, or locus.
   There was cellulitis at the site of the patient's previous incision.

6. **track** versus **tracked** versus **tract**

   track – Path, route; the path along which something moves, or the mark left by its movement (noun)/To follow the progress of (verb).
   The patient is on the right track for a full recovery.

   tracked – Past tense of track.
   We tracked the progress of the disease.

   tract – A region, usually one of some length; specifically a collection of nerve fibers or a number of organs, arranged in a series, serving a common function.
   There was no thickening of the fistulous tract.

I. MATCHING.
Match the correct term to the definition.

1. ____ silicone
2. ____ sight
3. ____ scarpus
4. ____ site
5. ____ track
6. ____ Scarpa's
7. ____ tract
8. ____ root
9. ____ silicon
10. ____ route

A. the lowermost portion
B. nonmetallic element
C. a location
D. path
E. channel
F. organic compound
G. seeing
H. a region
I. deep membranous layer
J. not a real word

II. MULTIPLE CHOICE.
Select the best answer.

1. The catheter was entered via left subclavian (◯ root, ◯ route).

2. The (◯ sight, ◯ site) of the patient's scar was severely edematous.

3. A cyst was noted just inferior to (◯ Scarpa's, ◯ scarpus) fascia.

4. The patient had recent (◯ silicon, ◯ silicone) breast implantation performed.

5. The patient's (◯ sight, ◯ site) was very poor secondary to cataracts.

6. The aortic (◯ root, ◯ route) appeared within normal limits.

7. The sinus (◯ track, ◯ tracked, ◯ tract) was clear of obstruction.

8. The compound was tested for (◯ silicon, ◯ silicone).

9. Laboratory values were (◯ track, ◯ tracked, ◯ tract) throughout the hospital course.

Word Differentiation – Lesson 14

1. **turbid** versus **turgid**

   turbid – Cloudy, unclear, as a liquid, or hazy air. Showing turbidity.
   The bottle had been shaken, and its contents were turbid as a result.

turgid – Swollen or congested. Having turgor or turgescence.
The edema caused the tissues to be turgid.

2. **uncal** versus **ungual** versus **lingual**

    uncal – Pertaining to the uncus (any hook-shaped structure; the medially curved anterior end of the parahippocampal gyrus).
    There is narrowing of the uncovertebral joint.

    ungual – Pertaining to the nails (fingernails and toenails).
    There was subungual swelling noted on musculoskeletal examination.

    lingual – Pertaining to or towards the tongue.
    The patient was instructed to take sublingual nitroglycerin p.r.n.

3. **vertex** versus **vortex**

    vertex – Summit or top; the top or crown of the head.
    Obstetrical ultrasound showed the fetus to be in vertex presentation.

    vortex – A whorled arrangement, design, or pattern, as of muscle fibers, or of the ridges or hairs on the skin.
    The patient had a vortex pattern on the ends of his fingers.

4. **viscus** versus **viscous**

    viscus – A large internal organ of the body. Especially one located in the great cavity of the trunk.
    The heart is a viscus as is the liver, spleen, or gallbladder.

    viscous – Descriptive word for a liquid that is thick and slow-flowing.
    Viscous lidocaine was given for anesthesia.

5. **waist** versus **waste**

    waist – The portion of the body between the thorax and the hips; a part resembling the human waist especially in narrowness or central position.
    The waist of the scaphoid was intact.

    waste – Gradual loss, decay, or diminution of bulk; damaged, defective, or superfluous material; refuse.
    There was wasting away of his muscle tissue.

6. **Xanax** versus **Zantac**

    Xanax – A drug used as a muscle relaxant and for anxiety disorders.
    The patient was prescribed Xanax for inability to sleep.

    Zantac – A drug used in the treatment of ulcers.
    The patient was put on Zantac and Milk of Magnesia.

I. MATCHING.
Match the correct term to the definition.

1. ____ lingual
2. ____ vertex
3. ____ uncal
4. ____ Zantac
5. ____ viscous
6. ____ ungual
7. ____ waist
8. ____ Xanax
9. ____ waste
10. ____ vortex
11. ____ viscus

A. between the chest and hips
B. used for anxiety
C. hook-shaped (adj.)
D. summit or top
E. used for ulcers
F. gradual loss or decay
G. towards the tongue
H. a whorled design
I. pertaining to the nails
J. large organ
K. thick and slow-flowing

II. MULTIPLE CHOICE.
Select the best answer.

1. The skin pattern appeared in a (◯ vertex, ◯ vortex) pattern.

2. (◯ Xanax, ◯ Zantac) was prescribed for peptic ulcer disease.

3. The patient had her temperature taken (◯ subuncally, ◯ subungually, ◯ sublingually).

4. Amniotic fluid is normal and the fetus is in a (◯ vertex, ◯ vortex) presentation.

5. The patient had gradual (◯ waisting, ◯ wasting) away of his mental capacities.

6. The patient was placed on (◯ Xanax, ◯ Zantac) following her violent rage.

7. A pin was jammed into the (◯ subuncal, ◯ subungual, ◯ sublingual) region, and it necessitated the removal of the nail.

8. She is unable to bend at the (◯ waist, ◯ waste).

9. The (◯ uncal, ◯ ungual) structure was normal on the cervical spine x-ray.

10. During surgery care was taken to avoid damage to any (◯ viscus, ◯ viscous).

11. Upon cutting into the brain during the autopsy, a (◯ viscus, ◯ viscous) fluid oozed out.

Review: Lessons 8-14

I. MATCHING.
Match the correct term to the definition.

1. ____ residents
2. ____ ostial
3. ____ lingual
4. ____ residence
5. ____ osteal
6. ____ prostrate
7. ____ uncal
8. ____ prostate
9. ____ resonance
10. ____ ungual

A. extended in a horizontal position
B. pertaining to the uncus
C. pertaining to an ostium (a door or opening)
D. pertaining to or towards the tongue
E. a gland in the male that surrounds the neck of the bladder and the urethra
F. pertaining to the nails (fingernails and toenails)
G. the place where one lives
H. bony, osseous
I. those who live in a place; physicians serving in residency
J. the prolongation and intensification of sound produced by the transmission of its vibrations to a cavity

II. MULTIPLE CHOICE.
Choose the best answer.

1. There was cellulitis at the (◯site, ◯sight) of the patient's previous incision.

2. We (◯tracked, ◯tract) the progress of the disease.

3. The population of Finland is quite (◯homogeneous, ◯homogenous) while the population of the U.S. is not.

4. The patient is on the right (◯track, ◯tract) for a full recovery.

5. The patient has very poor (◯site, ◯sight) in his left eye.

6. The cochlea and (◯malleolus, ◯malleus) were entirely normal.

7. The medial (◯malleolus, ◯malleus) was intact.

8. There was no thickening of the fistulous (◯tracked, ◯tract).

9. Informed consent (◯proceeded, ◯preceded) the procedure.

10. There was (◯homogeneous, ◯homogenous) echotexture throughout the kidney.

Unit 6
Abbreviations

Abbreviations – Introduction

In medical reports there is a lot of repetition. Specifically, all over the world, people have the same body parts, the same symptoms, acquire the same diseases and syndromes, have the same tests performed, and have similar laboratory values. As a result, many of these terms and phrases have come to be known by their respective abbreviations.

You will be more productive and efficient as a medical coder/biller if you are familiar with the most common medical abbreviations. The abbreviations you will study in this material do not include **all** of the abbreviations used in medical documents—that would require hundreds or possibly thousands of pages—but what is included here will serve as a good foundation.

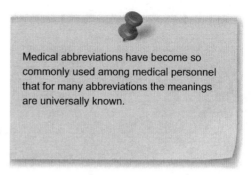

Medical abbreviations have become so commonly used among medical personnel that for many abbreviations the meanings are universally known.

Please notice that we are using "abbreviation" as a catch-all term to describe shortened or abbreviated forms of words or phrases. This unit actually covers four different types of abbreviated or shortened forms referred to as "abbreviations" for simplicity. These are:

1. **An abbreviation that is the shortened form of a longer word**: "exam" rather than "examination," for example, or "path" for "pathology," or "Jan" for "January." Some of these are acceptable in medical reports; others are not.

2. **An acronym, which consists of the initial letters of each word in the unabbreviated term**: "ACL" for "anterior cruciate ligament," "MI" for "myocardial infarction," "COPD" for "chronic obstructive pulmonary disease." These are nearly always presented in all capital letters, as shown. This form of abbreviation appears very commonly in medical documents.

3. **An acronym that is pronounced as though it were a spelled word:** "cabbage" for "CABG" (coronary artery bypass grafting), "leema" for "LIMA" (left internal mammary artery), or "haida" for "HIDA" (hepatoiminodiacetic acid or hydroxyiminodiacetic acid) scan. In all of these cases, however the term is pronounced, it is written as the proper acronymic abbreviation.

4. **Abbreviations (primarily from the Latin terms) for drug dosage instructions**: "b.i.d." for "twice daily," "p.r.n." for "as needed," "q.h.s." for "at bedtime," "p.o." for "by mouth."

Abbreviations In Our Culture

Abbreviations are part of our culture today like never before! Consider modern forms of communication—text messaging, instant messaging, e-mails and their new "abbreviated" language.

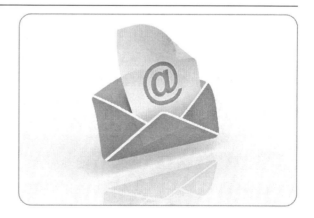

TMI — Too much information

ROFL — Rolling on the Floor, Laughing

BRB — Be Right Back

IMAO — In My Arrogant Opinion

L8R — Later

As you learned in previous modules, the purpose of using classification systems is to accurately describe and classify diagnoses and treatments. As a result, medical coders don't enjoy the luxury of dealing in "quick" or "shortened" forms. Medical coders need to have precise, unambiguous terms to accurately code.

One resource book entitled *Medical Abbreviations: 15,000 Conveniences at the Expense of Communications and Safety*, by Neil M. Davis summarizes the impact with the use of short cuts:

Abbreviations are a convenience, a time saver, a space saver, and a way of avoiding the possibility of misspelling words. However, a price can be paid for their use. Abbreviations are sometimes not understood, misread, or are interpreted incorrectly. Their use lengthens the time needed to train individuals in the health fields, wastes the time of healthcare workers in tracking down their meaning, at times delays the patient's care, and occasionally results in patient harm.

Although these are very real concerns, it is unlikely the medical world is going to quit using abbreviations any time in the foreseeable future. As a medical coder, you will find yourself making decisions about how to expand abbreviations and spending time, as Mr. Davis says, "tracking down [word] meaning" so you can accurately code patient records. Time and effort in the abbreviations unit will build your abbreviations medical vocabulary and prepare you to tackle the abbreviations challenge on the job. RTGS*?

Highlights

Medical coders need to have precise, unambiguous terms to accurately code.

Ready to Get Started?

Physical Examination – Lesson 1

In almost every type of report you will encounter, there will be a patient examination performed. The basic elements of the physical examination are the same regardless of what problem the patient has. The next few lessons contain some common abbreviations associated with the physical examination.

I. **ENTER ABBREVIATIONS.**
   Enter the abbreviation and what it stands for.

   A&P: auscultation and percussion
   1. _____ (Abbreviation)
   2. _____

   BP: blood pressure
   3. _____ (Abbreviation)
   4. _____

   CCE: clubbing, cyanosis, or edema
   5. _____ (Abbreviation)
   6. _____

   CNS: central nervous system
   7. _____ (Abbreviation)
   8. _____

CVA: costovertebral angle

9. _____ (Abbreviation)

10. _____

II. FILL IN THE BLANK.

Read the following history and physical excerpts. Enter the appropriate abbreviation for the bolded expansion.

1. Vital signs showed temperature 102.8 rectally, respiratory rate 52, pulse 176, and **blood pressure** of 104/73.

   _____

2. Motor: Normal tone and strength, no deficits. Cranial nerves 2-12 are intact. **Central nervous system** is within normal limits.

   _____

3. Chest is symmetric. No trauma or contusions noted. Lungs clear to **auscultation and percussion**. _____

4. At the time of the examination, the patient is not in respiratory distress. There are minimal crackles heard on lung examination. Respiratory rate is 15. Examination of the upper extremities reveals no **clubbing, cyanosis or edema**. Mucous membranes are moist. _____

5. Spine has a normal lordotic curve. There is no **costovertebral angle** tenderness. No pain with lateral side bending.

   _____

auscultation and percussion
blood pressure
clubbing, cyanosis, or edema
central nervous system
costovertebral angle

III. FILL IN THE BLANK.

Use the word(s) in the box to expand the bolded abbreviations in the following sentences.

1. His vital signs showed a **BP** of 110/73. _____

2. There was no **CCE** on examination of the extremities.

   _____

3. Chest: Clear to **A&P**. _____

4. She had no **CVA** tenderness. _____

5. **CNS** is within normal limits. _____

I. **ENTER ABBREVIATIONS.**
Enter the abbreviation and what it stands for.

DTR: deep tendon reflex

1. _____ (Abbreviation)

2. _____

EOMI: extraocular movements (or muscles) intact

3. _____ (Abbreviation)

4. _____

GI: gastrointestinal

5. _____ (Abbreviation)

6. _____

GU: genitourinary

7. _____ (Abbreviation)

8. _____

HEENT: head, eyes, ears, nose and throat

9. _____ (Abbreviation)

10. _____

IAC: internal auditory canal

11. _____ (Abbreviation)

12. _____

JVD: jugular venous distention

13. _____ (Abbreviation)

14. _____

*Most commonly seen in plural form DTRs or deep tendon reflexes.

II. FILL IN THE BLANK.

Read the following history and physical excerpts. Enter the appropriate abbreviation for the bolded expansion.

1. **Gastrointestinal** exam revealed the abdomen was soft, nontender. Bowel sounds present in all four quadrants. No hepatosplenomegaly or masses. _____

2. Pupils equal and reactive to light. **Extraocular movements intact**. Tympanic membranes were noted to be gray and mobile. _____

3. Extremities revealed the ankles were plantar flexed with somewhat increased tone. **Deep tendon reflexes** revealed 1+ in the upper extremities and 2+ in the lower extremities. *Hint: Note the plural form.* _____

4. Nose had a clear discharge. Throat was clear. Mucous membranes were moist. Neck was supple. No **jugular venous distention**. No carotid bruits noted. _____

5. **Head, eyes, ears, nose and throat**: Normocephalic, atraumatic. Anterior fontanelle was soft. Tympanic membranes were pink and mobile. _____

6. The patient was a well-developed, well-nourished male accompanied by his mother. HEENT revealed a normal exam except for PE (pressure equalization) tubes present in both ears. The **internal auditory canal** on the right side showed some redness and irritation.

   _____

7. Stent tubing was noted extending from his abdomen and this had been clamped. His **genitourinary** exam was unremarkable. _____

III. **FILL IN THE BLANK.**
Use the word(s) in the box to expand the bolded abbreviations in the following sentences.

1. Neck showed no **JVD**. _____

2. **GU** exam was within normal limits. _____

3. **HEENT** exam was normal. _____

4. **DTRs** intact. _____ *Hint: Use the plural*

   expansion.

5. Sclerae anicteric. **EOMI**. _____

6. **GI**: Abdomen soft, nontender. _____

7. **IAC** on the left was impacted with cerumen. _____

extraocular muscles intact
internal auditory canal
jugular venous distention
gastrointestinal
head, eyes, ears, nose and throat
genitourinary
deep tendon reflexes

Physical Examination – Lesson 3

I. **ENTER ABBREVIATIONS.**
Enter the abbreviation and what it stands for.

JVP: jugular venous pressure
1. _____ (Abbreviation)
2. _____

NAD: no acute distress
3. _____ (Abbreviation)
4. _____

NC/AT: normocephalic, atraumatic
5. _____ (Abbreviation)
6. _____

OD: right eye
7. _____ (Abbreviation)
8. _____

OS: left eye
9. _____ (Abbreviation)
10. _____

II. FILL IN THE BLANK.
Read the following history and physical excerpts. Enter the appropriate abbreviation for the bolded expansion.

1. Eyes: Cataract **right eye**. The remainder of the eye examination is within normal limits.

   _____

2. The patient was alert and oriented to time, place and person, in **no acute distress**.

   _____

3. Neck: normal **jugular venous pressure**. There is no stiffness or pain on palpation.

   _____

4. To resolve the irritation, she was instructed to place 2 drops of ophthalmic solution in the **left eye** every 4 hours. _____

5. Head: **normocephalic, atraumatic**. No scalp tenderness. Pupils are equal and reactive to light and accommodation. _____

III. FILL IN THE BLANK.
Use the word(s) in the box to expand the bolded abbreviations in the following sentences.

1. The patient was alert and oriented, in **NAD**. _____

2. Eyes: **OD** _____

3. Eyes: **OS** _____

4. The head was **NC/AT**. _____

5. On neck exam, the **JVP** was normal. _____

normocephalic, atraumatic
jugular venous pressure
left eye
no acute distress
right eye

Physical Examination – Lesson 4

I. ENTER ABBREVIATIONS.
Enter the abbreviation and what it stands for.

PERRLA: pupils equal, round, reactive to light and accommodation

1. _____ (Abbreviation)
2. _____

PMI: point of maximal impulse

3. _____ (Abbreviation)

4. _____

REM: rapid eye movement

5. _____ (Abbreviation)

6. _____

ROM: range of motion

7. _____ (Abbreviation)

8. _____

TM: tympanic membrane

9. _____ (Abbreviation)

10. _____

II. **FILL IN THE BLANK.**
Read the following history and physical excerpts. Enter in the appropriate abbreviation for the bolded expansion.

1. Vital signs were within normal limits. Examination of the head, ears, eyes, nose and throat: **pupils equal, round, reactive to light and accommodation.** _____

2. Ears: **tympanic membrane** pearly grey. No bulging or irritation. _____

3. Chest: **point of maximal impulse** within normal limits. No murmurs, rubs or gallops. No tenderness, normal lung expansion. _____

4. During the sleep phase of the encephalogram, **rapid eye movement** was noted.

_____

5. Back examination, **range of motion** testing revealed some stiffness on forward flexion. Otherwise there were no complaints of pain or tenderness. _____

III. FILL IN THE BLANK.
Use the word(s) in the box to expand the bolded abbreviations in the following sentences.

1. The **TM** in both ears is clear. _____

2. Left leg showed **ROM** intact. _____

3. Examination of the head, ears, eyes, nose and throat: **PERRLA**.

   _____

4. On sleep test, **REM** was noted. _____

5. The **PMI** was intact. _____

point of maximal impulse
range of motion
tympanic membrane
rapid eye movement
pupils equal, round, reactive to light and accommodation

Review: Physical Examination

I. FILL IN THE BLANK.
Enter the correct abbreviation or its long form in the blank provided.

1. Internal auditory canal _____

2. CCE _____

3. Point of Maximal impulse _____

4. extraocular movements (or muscles) intact _____

5. TM _____

6. genitourinary _____

7. NAD _____

8. left eye _____

9. HEENT _____

10. ROM _____

II. MULTIPLE CHOICE.
Choose the correct abbreviation.

1. auscultation and percussion (◯A&P, ◯AP)

2. costovertebral angle (◯CVA, ◯CA)

3. internal auditory canal (◯ACI, ◯IAC)

4. gastrointestinal (◯GN, ◯GI)

5. deep tendon reflex (◯DTR, ◯DR)

6. normocephalic, atraumatic (◯N/A, ◯NC/AT)

7. rapid eye movement (◯REM, ◯RE)

8. right eye (◯OD, ◯OS)

Physical Examination Abbreviations List

Abbreviation	Expansion
A&P	auscultation and percussion
BP	blood pressure
CCE	clubbing, cyanosis, or edema
CNS	central nervous system
CVA	costovertebral angle
DTR	deep tendon reflex
EOMI	extraocular movements intact or extraocular muscles intact
GI	gastrointestinal
GU	genitourinary
HEENT	head, eyes, ears, nose, and throat
IAC	internal auditory canal
JVD	jugular venous distention
JVP	jugular venous pressure
NAD	no acute distress
NC/AT	normocephalic/atraumatic
OD	right eye
OS	left eye
PERRLA	pupils equal, round, reactive to light and accommodation
PMI	point of maximal impulse
REM	rapid eye movements
ROM	range of motion
TM	tympanic membrane

Laboratory Data – Lesson 1

Laboratory data and abbreviations go hand in hand. In fact, there isn't a section in medical reports where you are more likely to encounter abbreviations than in the laboratory section. Commonly accepted style guides for creating medical reports often allow the use of laboratory abbreviations in the diagnosis list and procedure list, while the use of other abbreviations in those sections is frowned upon.

Laboratory data can look like secret code—filled with numbers, acronyms, and abbreviations.

Example: H and H 7.5 and 42.1 with MCV 88.4, platelets 154.

The upside is that laboratory abbreviations are used so commonly they are generally easy to find and verify in their abbreviated forms in reference books and laboratory resources. Careful study of this section will help you decipher laboratory data—which otherwise might look like secret code!

I. ENTER ABBREVIATIONS.
Enter the abbreviation and what it stands for.

ABG: arterial blood gas*

1. _____ (Abbreviation)

2. _____

Plural form ABGs, arterial blood gases.

AFB: acid-fast bacillus

3. _____ (Abbreviation)

4. _____

BUN: blood urea nitrogen

5. _____ (Abbreviation)

6. _____

CBC: complete blood count

7. _____ (Abbreviation)

8. _____

CO2: carbon dioxide

9. _____ (Abbreviation)

10. _____

C&S: culture and sensitivity

11. _____ (Abbreviation)

12. _____

II. **FILL IN THE BLANK.**
   Read the following excerpts and enter the appropriate abbreviation for the bolded expansion.

   1. **Arterial blood gases** showed a pH of 7.32, a pCO2 of 24, and a saturation of 93%. *(Hint: Plural form.)*_____

   2. Results from the sputum culture revealed the tuberculosis pathogen is **acid-fast bacillus**.

      _____

   3. **Blood urea nitrogen** is 12, creatinine is 2.6._____

   4. The **complete blood count** revealed a hemoglobin of 12 and hematocrit of 36, White count 8700._____

   5. Blood gases on room air revealed a **carbon dioxide** of 13._____

   6. **Culture and sensitivity** of the urine specimen revealed abnormal pathogens.

      _____

III. **FILL IN THE BLANK.**
   Use the word(s) in the box to expand the bolded abbreviations in the following sentences.

   1. **CO2** was 13. _____

   2. Creatinine was 2.2 and **BUN** was 12.8. _____

   3. A **CBC** was drawn and was within normal limits.

      _____

   4. **ABG** revealed a pH of 7.33. _____

   5. **C&S** was done. _____

   6. A smear for **AFB** was negative. _____

culture and sensitivity
carbon dioxide
acid-fast bacillus
complete blood count
blood urea nitrogen
arterial blood gas

Laboratory Data – Lesson 2

I. **ENTER ABBREVIATIONS.**
   Enter the abbreviation and what it stands for.

   CSF: cerebrospinal fluid
   1. _____ (Abbreviation)
   2. _____

FEV: forced expiratory volume
    3. _____ (Abbreviation)
    4. _____

FVC: forced vital capacity
    5. _____ (Abbreviation)
    6. _____

GTT: glucose tolerance test
    7. _____ (Abbreviation)
    8. _____

H&H: hemoglobin and hematocrit
    9. _____ (Abbreviation)
    10. _____

HIV: human immunodeficiency virus
    11. _____ (Abbreviation)
    12. _____

KCl: potassium chloride
    13. _____ (Abbreviation)
    14. _____

LFT: liver function test
    15. _____ (Abbreviation)
    16. _____

II. **FILL IN THE BLANK.**
Read the following excerpts and enter the appropriate abbreviation for the bolded expansion.

    1. The **cerebrospinal fluid** was cloudy and turbid. A sample was sent to Pathology for assessment. _____

    2. Blood gases revealed a **forced expiratory volume** of 40 when checked with incentive spirometry._____

    3. The **forced vital capacity** was also checked using the incentive spirometer._____

    4. The **glucose tolerance test** was found to be elevated on this fasting specimen. This will require additional workup._____

5. The complete blood count revealed a **hemoglobin and hematocrit** of 12 and 36 respectively.

   _____

6. The clinic routinely carries out **human immunodeficiency virus** testing without charge to those who wish it._____

7. The **potassium chloride** level was found to be elevated during routine blood work.

   _____

8. The patient appeared minimally jaundiced and had abnormal **liver function tests**. These will be repeated and appropriate therapy instituted._____

III. **FILL IN THE BLANK.**
   Use the choices in the box below to expand the abbreviation bolded in the following sentences.

   1. His **LFTs** were within normal limits. _____

   2. CBC showed an **H&H** of 13.7 and 37.9. _____

   3. She had negative **HIV** testing. _____

   4. **CSF** was obtained, the results of which were within normal limits. _____

   5. The patient underwent a pulmonary function test with results showing **FVC** within normal range. _____

   6. The patient underwent a **GTT** to check for diabetes.

      _____

human immunodeficiency virus
potassium chloride
liver function tests
forced vital capacity
cerebrospinal fluid
glucose tolerance test
hemoglobin and hematocrit

   7. The patient's medications included **KCl** for electrolyte balance while using the Dyazide. _____

Laboratory Data – Lesson 3

I. **ENTER ABBREVIATIONS.**
   Enter the abbreviation and what it stands for.

   LP: lumbar puncture

   1. _____ (Abbreviation)

   2. _____

O&P: ova and parasites

3. _____ (Abbreviation)

4. _____

PFT: pulmonary function test

5. _____ (Abbreviation)

6. _____

PSA: prostate-specific antigen

7. _____ (Abbreviation)

8. _____

PT: prothrombin time

9. _____ (Abbreviation)

10. _____

PTT: partial thromboplastin time

11. _____ (Abbreviation)

12. _____

II. **FILL IN THE BLANK.**
Read the following excerpts and enter the appropriate abbreviation for the bolded expansion.

1. After nebulization, **pulmonary function tests** were repeated. *Hint: Plural form.*

_____

2. International normalized ratio is 3.5, **prothrombin time** 28.2. _____

3. Because of the neurological symptoms, a **lumbar puncture** was obtained and was negative.

_____

4. **Prostate-specific antigen** was drawn today and is 7.3, which is consistent with prior values.

_____

5. Automated complete blood count: White count was 5.8, hemoglobin 14.2, platelets 238. **Partial thromboplastin time** was essentially normal. _____

6. As part of the workup for ongoing diarrhea, stool sample was taken for **ova and parasites**.

_____

FILL IN THE BLANK.
Use the word(s) in the box to expand the bolded abbreviations in the following sentences.

1. **PT** was checked and is 13.6. _____

2. **PTT** was checked and is 29.2. _____

3. Local anesthesia was administered and then a 22-gauge spinal needle was passed into the lumbar subarachnoid space and a **LP** was performed. _____

4. **O&P** were negative. _____

5. He had **PFTs** done, which revealed a forced expiratory volume of 2.09, which improved to 2.33 with bronchodilators (or a 23% change.) _____

6. **PSA** is a very helpful test to screen for prostate cancer.

_____

partial thromboplastin time
pulmonary function tests
prostate-specific antigen
prothrombin time
lumbar puncture
ova and parasites

Laboratory Data – Lesson 4

I. **ENTER ABBREVIATIONS.**
Enter the abbreviation and what it stands for.

RBC*: red blood count or red blood cell

1. _____ (Abbreviation)
2. _____

RPR: rapid plasma reagin

3. _____ (Abbreviation)
4. _____

SMA: sequential multichannel autoanalyzer or simultaneous multichannel autoanalyzer

5. _____ (Abbreviation)
6. _____

TB: tuberculosis

7. _____ (Abbreviation)
8. _____

UA: urinalysis

    9. _____ (Abbreviation)

   10. _____

WBC*: white blood count or white blood cell

   11. _____ (Abbreviation)

   12. _____

*Expansion depends on the context. Read carefully to determine which expansion is appropriate.

II. FILL IN THE BLANK.
Read the following excerpts and enter the appropriate abbreviation for the bolded expansion.

1. As part of her workup, the family physician requested she have a **red blood count** done at the local laboratory. _____

2. The **rapid plasma reagin** was drawn because of a generalized rash in the genital area.

   _____

3. The **sequential multichannel autoanalyzer** was essentially within normal limits when drawn at the time of admission to the hospital. _____

4. Because of recent exposure to infected family members, a **tuberculosis** skin test was performed. _____

5. The clean catch **urinalysis** revealed white cells too numerous to count, red blood cells and some bacteria. _____

6. The complete blood count showed a **white blood count** of 8000. _____

7. Automated complete blood count: **White blood cells** 3.4, red blood cells 3.76, hemoglobin 9.8, hematocrit 28.3. _____

8. Complete blood count: White blood cells 3.4, **red blood cells** 3.76, hemoglobin 9.8, hematocrit 28.3. *Hint: Plural form.* _____

III. FILL IN THE BLANK.
Use the word(s) in the box to expand the bolded abbreviations in the following sentences.

1. Her urinalysis showed no **WBCs**. *Hint: Plural form.*

   _____

2. The patient's condition was suspicious for acid-fast bacillus infection so a **TB** test was ordered. _____

3. She had no evidence of **RBCs** in the urine. *Hint: Plural form.*

   _____

4. She had a negative clean catch **UA**. _____

5. The physician suspected this patient to have syphilis so he was sent for screening with **RPR**. _____

6. In the emergency room the physician ordered a special laboratory panel called an **SMA**. _____

7. Automated complete blood count: **WBCs** 3.4, red blood cells 3.76, hemoglobin 9.8, hematocrit 28.3. _____

8. Complete blood count: White blood cells 3.4, **RBCs** 3.76, hemoglobin 9.8, hematocrit 28.3. _____

simultaneous multichannel autoanalyzer
tuberculosis
rapid plasma reagin
white blood cells
red blood cells
urinalysis

Review: Laboratory Data

I. FILL IN THE BLANK.
Enter the correct abbreviation or its long form in the blank provided.

1. culture and sensitivity _____

2. PT _____

3. BUN _____

4. carbon dioxide _____

5. CBC _____

6. forced vital capacity _____

7. human immunodeficiency virus _____

8. ABG _____

9. liver function test _____

10. GTT _____

II. MULTIPLE CHOICE.
Choose the correct abbreviation.

1. hemoglobin and hematocrit (◯HH, ◯H&H)

2. potassium chloride (◯PCl, ◯KCl)

3. prostate-specific antigen (◯PSA, ◯PA)

4. ova and parasites (◯OP, ◯O&P)

5. forced expiratory volume (◯FEV, ◯FExV)

6. acid-fast bacillus (◯AFB, ◯A-FB)

7. partial thromboplastin time (◯PTT, ◯PTPT)

8. cerebrospinal fluid (◯CF, ◯CSF)

Laboratory Data Abbreviations List

Abbreviation	Expansion
ABG	arterial blood gas
AFB	acid-fast bacillus
BUN	blood urea nitrogen
CBC	complete blood count
CO_2	carbon dioxide
C&S	culture and sensitivity
CSF	cerebrospinal fluid
FEV	forced expiratory volume
FVC	forced vital capacity
GTT	glucose tolerance test/drop
H&H	hemoglobin and hematocrit
HIV	human immunodeficiency virus

KCl	potassium chloride
LFT	liver function test
LP	lumbar puncture
O&P	ova and parasites
PFT	pulmonary function test
PSA	prostate specific antigen
PT	prothrombin time
PTT	partial thromboplastin time
RBC	red blood count or red blood cell
RPR	rapid plasma reagin
SMA	sequential multichannel autoanalyzer/simultaneous multichannel autoanalyzer
TB	tuberculosis
UA	urinalysis
WBC	white blood count or white blood cell

Diseases and Syndromes – Lesson 1

This lesson of abbreviations is both the most extensive and the most commonly used, aside from those seen in the laboratory data. The diseases that tend to be abbreviated are the ones that affect the largest number of people and are the most often treated. Studying and memorizing as many of these as you can will help you to be efficient and effective because you will not have to continuously search for correct abbreviation expansions.

I. **ENTER ABBREVIATIONS.**
   Enter the abbreviation and what it stands for.

   AAA: abdominal aortic aneurysm
   Upon exploration of the abdomen, no AAA was noted.

   1. _____ (Abbreviation)

   2. _____

   This particular abbreviation will often be dictated "triple A," but should always be typed AAA.

   AIDS: acquired immune deficiency syndrome
   The patient has AIDS, stage V.

   3. _____ (Abbreviation)

   4. _____

   AIDS is almost exclusively pronounced as the word its letters spell.

ALL: acute lymphocytic leukemia (acute lymphoblastic leukemia)
The patient has advanced ALL.

   5. _____ (Abbreviation)

   6. _____

   7. _____

ARDS: adult respiratory distress syndrome
She has known ARDS, with a long history of smoking.

   8. _____ (Abbreviation)

   9. _____

BPH: benign prostatic hypertrophy
On biopsy, he was found to have BPH.

   10. _____ (Abbreviation)

   11. _____

Benign prostatic hyperplasia is also an acceptable expansion of BPH.

II. FILL IN THE BLANK.
Use the word(s) above to fill in the blanks.

   1. She was admitted with a known history of adult _____ distress
      2. _____.

   3. He has known _____ immune 4. _____ syndrome.

   5. On prostate exam he was found to have benign prostatic _____.

   6. Acute _____ leukemia was diagnosed three months ago.

   7. She has an abdominal aortic _____.

III. FILL IN THE BLANK.
Expand the following abbreviations. For any abbreviation that has more than one expansion, just choose one that is appropriate for this lesson.

1. BPH _____   2. AIDS _____

3. AAA _____   4. ALL _____

5. ARDS _____

Diseases and Syndromes – Lesson 2

I. **ENTER ABBREVIATIONS.**
   Enter the abbreviation and what it stands for.

   CA: cancer or carcinoma
   The patient has a history of CA of the liver.

   1. _____ (Abbreviation)

   2. _____

   CF: cystic fibrosis
   He was hospitalized twice for his CF.

   3. _____ (Abbreviation)

   4. _____

   CHF: congestive heart failure
   He presented with CHF.

   5. _____ (Abbreviation)

   6. _____

   CMV: cytomegalovirus
   She was diagnosed with CMV.

   7. _____ (Abbreviation)

   8. _____

   COPD: chronic obstructive pulmonary disease
   He has a history of COPD.

   9. _____ (Abbreviation)

   10. _____

   CVA: cerebrovascular accident
   The patient presented to the emergency room with symptoms of CVA.

   11. _____ (Abbreviation)

   12. _____

   CVA also stands for costovertebral angle and is frequently dictated in the physical exam portion of a report.
   Make sure, by careful attention to context, that you use the correct one.

FILL IN THE BLANK.
   Use the word(s) above to fill in the blanks.

   1. She has adeno _____ of the kidneys.

   2. The patient has _____ pulmonary disease.

   3. He presented with _____ heart failure.

   4. A diagnosis of _____ fibrosis was made.

   5. On testing he was found to have suffered a _____ accident.

   6. Cyto_____ is his primary diagnosis.

III. **FILL IN THE BLANK.**
   Expand the following abbreviations. For any abbreviation that has more than one expansion, just choose one that is appropriate for this lesson.

   1. CMV _____   2. COPD _____

   3. CHF _____   4. CA _____

   5. CVA _____   6. CF _____

Diseases and Syndromes – Lesson 3

I. **ENTER ABBREVIATIONS.**
   Enter the abbreviation and what it stands for.

   DISH: diffuse idiopathic skeletal hyperostosis
   On skeletal survey he was found to have DISH.

   1. _____ (Abbreviation)

   2. _____

   The introduction to this chapter stated that there were two primary ways of dictating abbreviations. You have already had several examples of the first, namely, saying each individual letter. This is an example of the second method of dictating abbreviations. DISH is almost exclusively pronounced as the word its letters spell (dish—as in plate or bowl). There are other abbreviations that fall into this category, and they will be noted as they occur.

   DJD: degenerative joint disease
   He has DJD of the acromioclavicular joint.

   3. _____ (Abbreviation)

   4. _____

DM: diabetes mellitus
The patient's blood sugars are high, consistent with a history of DM.

   5. _____ (Abbreviation)

   6. _____

DVT: deep venous thrombosis (deep vein thrombosis)
The patient is on Coumadin for DVT.

   7. _____ (Abbreviation)

   8. _____

FCD: fibrocystic disease
On mammogram the breasts show a pattern consistent with FCD.

   9. _____ (Abbreviation)

  10. _____

II. FILL IN THE BLANK.
Use the word(s) above to fill in the blanks.

1. X-ray shows evidence of diffuse _____

   skeletal 2. _____.

3. Ultrasound of the leg showed deep venous _____.

4. _____ disease was noted on mammogram.

5. The patient takes insulin for her diabetes _____.

6. He has a history of _____ joint disease.

III. FILL IN THE BLANK.
Expand the following abbreviations. For any abbreviation that has more than one expansion, just choose one that is appropriate for this lesson.

1. DVT_____   2. DM_____

3. DJD_____   4. DISH_____

5. FCD_____

Diseases and Syndromes – Lesson 4

I. ENTER ABBREVIATIONS.
Enter the abbreviation and what it stands for.

GERD: gastroesophageal reflux disease
GI consulted and gave a diagnosis of GERD.

1. _____ (Abbreviation)

2. _____

HMD: hyaline membrane disease
The baby's ultrasound is consistent with HMD.

3. _____ (Abbreviation)

4. _____

HNP: herniated nucleus pulposus
He has HNP noted at L4-5.

5. _____ (Abbreviation)

6. _____

IDDM: insulin-dependent diabetes mellitus
His IDDM was poorly controlled.

7. _____ (Abbreviation)

8. _____

ILD: interstitial lung disease
Chest x-ray confirmed ILD.

9. _____ (Abbreviation)

10. _____

II. FILL IN THE BLANK.
Use the word(s) above to fill in the blanks.

1. Gastroesophageal _____ disease was noted.

2. _____ nucleus 3. _____ at C3-4.

4. _____ lung disease is present.

5. She takes NPH for her _____ diabetes mellitus.

6. Her _____ membrane disease is a result of prematurity.

III. **FILL IN THE BLANK.**
   Expand the following abbreviations. For any abbreviation that has more than one expansion, just choose one that is appropriate for this lesson

   1. HMD_____   2. GERD_____

   3. IDDM_____   4. HNP_____

   5. ILD_____

Diseases and Syndromes – Lesson 5

I. **ENTER ABBREVIATIONS.**
   Enter the abbreviation and what it stands for.

   MS: multiple sclerosis
   Her multiple sclerosis precluded general anesthetic.

   1. _____ (Abbreviation)

   2. _____

   PTSD: post-traumatic stress disorder
   The veteran suffered from PTSD.

   3. _____ (Abbreviation)

   4. _____

   RA: rheumatoid arthritis
   Findings compatible with rheumatoid arthritis.

   5. _____ (Abbreviation)

   6. _____

   RSD: reflex sympathetic dystrophy
   The patient has known RSD.

   7. _____ (Abbreviation)

   8. _____

   RSV: respiratory syncytial virus
   He was diagnosed with RSV pneumonia.

   9. _____ (Abbreviation)

   10. _____

II. FILL IN THE BLANK.
Use the word(s) above to fill in the blanks.

1. She was diagnosed with multiple _____.

2. Severe _____ arthritis can cause deformity of the joints.

3. The patient has a history of reflex sympathetic _____.

4. Respiratory _____ virus was the primary diagnosis.

5. _____ stress disorder was evident.

III. FILL IN THE BLANK.
Expand the following abbreviations. For any abbreviation that has more than one expansion, just choose one that is appropriate for this lesson.

1. MS _____   2. PTSD _____

3. RSV _____   4. RA _____

5. RSD _____

Diseases and Syndromes – Lesson 6

I. ENTER ABBREVIATIONS.
Enter the abbreviation and what it stands for.

SIDS: sudden infant death syndrome
The autopsy was negative, suggesting a diagnosis of SIDS.

1. _____ (Abbreviation)

2. _____

SIDS is almost exclusively pronounced as the word its letters spell.

SLE: systemic lupus erythematosus
The symptoms point to a diagnosis of SLE.

3. _____ (Abbreviation)

4. _____

TIA: transient ischemic attack
The patient has a history of chronic TIAs.

5. _____ (Abbreviation)

6. _____

URI: upper respiratory infection
With negative strep, URI is the most likely diagnosis.

    7. _____ (Abbreviation)

    8. _____

UTI: urinary tract infection
She has a long history of UTIs.

    9. _____ (Abbreviation)

    10. _____

II. FILL IN THE BLANK.
Use the word(s) above to fill in the blanks.

1. He presented to the ER last week with an upper _____ infection.

2. Cause of death was _____ lupus [3.] _____.

4. He was admitted for a transient _____.

5. She was given antibiotics for a _____ tract [6.] _____.

7. The baby died of _____ infant death [8.] _____.

III. FILL IN THE BLANK.
Expand the following abbreviations. For any abbreviation that has more than one expansion, just choose one that is appropriate for this lesson.

1. TIA _____

2. UTI _____

3. SLE _____

4. URI _____

5. SIDS _____

Review: Diseases and Syndromes

I. FILL IN THE BLANK.
Some spaces may require more than one word. Be sure to provide the complete answer. For any question that may have more than one appropriate answer, just choose one.

1. degenerative _____ disease

2. _____ vascular accident

3. chronic _____ disease

4. sudden infant _____

5. _____ ischemic attack

6. congestive heart _____

7. upper _____ infection

8. deep _____

9. _____ tract infection

10. diffuse _____ hyperostosis

cerebro
death syndrome
failure
idiopathic skeletal
joint
obstructive pulmonary
respiratory
transient
urinary
venous thrombosis

II. MATCHING.
Match the word or word part to the abbreviation expansion. You may use each answer more than once, or not at all.

1. ____ UTI – urinary tract _____

2. ____ RA – rheumatoid _____

3. ____ CMV – _____ virus

4. ____ DM – diabetes _____

5. ____ HMD – hyaline _____ disease

6. ____ RSV – respiratory _____ virus

7. ____ PTSD – post-traumatic _____ disorder

8. ____ DVT – deep venous _____

9. ____ CA – _____

10. ____ TIA – _____ ischemic attack

A. cytomegalo
B. syncytial
C. thrombosis
D. carcinoma
E. transient
F. mellitus
G. infection
H. arthritis
I. stress
J. membrane

Choose the correct word or word part for the abbreviation expansion.

1. SLE – systemic lupus (◯erythematous, ◯ erythematosus)

2. FCD – fibro (◯chronic, ◯ cystic) disease

3. RSD – reflex (◯sympathetic, ◯ systemic) dystrophy

4. HNP – herniated nucleus (◯pulposus, ◯ pulpous)

5. GERD – gastroesophageal (◯reflex, ◯ reflux) disease

6. ILD – (◯innerstitial, ◯ interstitial) lung disease

7. CHF – (◯congestive, ◯ cardiac) heart failure

8. DJD – degenerative joint (◯disorder, ◯ disease)

9. MS – (◯megalo, ◯ multiple) sclerosis

10. CF – (◯cerebral, ◯ cystic) fibrosis

Diseases and Syndromes Abbreviations List

Abbreviation	Expansion
AAA	abdominal aortic aneurysm
AIDS	acquired immune deficiency syndrome
ALL	acute lymphocytic leukemia or acute lymphoblastic leukemia
ARDS	adult respiratory distress syndrome
BPH	benign prostatic hypertrophy
CA	cancer or carcinoma
CF	cystic fibrosis
CHF	congestive heart failure
CMV	cytomegalovirus
COPD	chronic obstructive pulmonary disease
CVA	cerebrovascular accident
DISH	diffuse idiopathic skeletal hyperostosis
DJD	degenerative joint disease
DM	diabetes mellitus
DVT	deep venous thrombosis

FCD	fibrocystic disease
GERD	gastroesophageal reflux disease
HMD	hyaline membrane disease
HNP	herniated nucleus pulposus
IDDM	insulin-dependent diabetes mellitus
ILD	interstitial lung disease
MS	multiple sclerosis
PTSD	post-traumatic stress disorder
RA	rheumatoid arthritis
RSD	reflex sympathetic dystrophy
RSV	respiratory syncytial virus
SIDS	sudden infant death syndrome
SLE	systemic lupus erythematosus
TIA	transient ischemic attack
URI	upper respiratory infection
UTI	urinary tract infection

Surgery – Lesson 1

I. **ENTER ABBREVIATIONS.**
Enter the abbreviation and what it stands for.

AKA: above-knee amputation
Examination of the lower extremities revealed a right AKA.

1. _____ (Abbreviation)

2. _____

BKA: below-knee amputation
History of BKA in 1969.

3. _____ (Abbreviation)

4. _____

CTR: carpal tunnel release
Her carpal tunnel syndrome will require CTR.

5. _____ (Abbreviation)

6. _____

EBL: estimated blood loss
EBL: 200 cc.

    7. _____ (Abbreviation)

    8. _____

EGD: esophagogastroduodenoscopy
EGD revealed no lesions.

    9. _____ (Abbreviation)

    10. _____

II. FILL IN THE BLANK.
Use the word(s) above to fill in the blanks.

1. He had a below-knee _____ performed.

2. Carpal _____ release was scheduled.

3. GI performed an _____.

4. _____ blood loss was minimal.

5. An above-_____ amputation was performed at another facility.

III. FILL IN THE BLANK.
Expand the following abbreviations. For any abbreviation that has more than one expansion, just choose one that is appropriate for this lesson.

1. EBL_____   2. AKA_____

3. BKA_____   4. CTR_____

5. EGD_____

Surgery – Lesson 2

I. ENTER ABBREVIATIONS.
Enter the abbreviation and what it stands for.

ET: endotracheal (usually tube)
Anesthesia was general ET tube.

    1. _____ (Abbreviation)

    2. _____

I&D: incision and drainage
He was admitted for I&D of his infected wound.

    3. _____ (Abbreviation)

    4. _____

IJ: internal jugular
The line was placed via a right IJ approach.

    5. _____ (Abbreviation)

    6. _____

IM: intramuscular
IM medicines were administered.

    7. _____ (Abbreviation)

    8. _____

IV: intravenous
He was started on IV antibiotics.

    9. _____ (Abbreviation)

    10. _____

II. FILL IN THE BLANK.
Use the word(s) above to fill in the blanks.

1. For administration of medications, _____ venous line was started.

2. The administration of intra_____ drugs was ordered.

3. Anesthesia was per _____ tube.

4. The catheter was inserted via a left internal _____ approach.

5. He had an _____ and 6._____ of his infected right knee abscess.

III. FILL IN THE BLANK.
Expand the following abbreviations. For any abbreviation that has more than one expansion, just choose one that is appropriate for this lesson.

1. IV_____   2. ET_____

3. IM_____   4. I&D_____

5. IJ_____

Surgery – Lesson 3

I. ENTER ABBREVIATIONS.
Enter the abbreviation and what it stands for.

lap: laparotomy or laparoscopic
Lap cholecystectomy was performed.

   1. _____ (Abbreviation)

   2. _____

LR: lactated Ringer's
1,000 cc LR was administered.

   3. _____ (Abbreviation)

   4. _____

K-wire: Kirschner wire
A K-wire was used for fixation.

   5. _____ (Abbreviation)

   6. _____

NG: nasogastric (usually tube)
An NG tube was inserted.

   7. _____ (Abbreviation)

   8. _____

ORIF: open reduction, internal fixation
He was taken to the OR where ORIF was performed of the ankle fracture.

   9. _____ (Abbreviation)

   10. _____

II. FILL IN THE BLANK.
Use the word(s) above to fill in the blanks.

   1. Open _____ internal [2.]_____ of the fracture was performed.

   3. A _____ tube was inserted for feedings.

   4. _____ wire fixation was utilized.

   5. She failed _____cholecystectomy, and open procedure was undertaken.

   6. The patient was administered 1500 cc lactated _____.

FILL IN THE BLANK.
   Expand the following abbreviations. For any abbreviation that has more than one expansion, just choose one that is appropriate for this lesson.

   1. NG_____   2. ORIF_____

   3. LR_____   4. K-wire_____

   5. lap_____

Surgery – Lesson 4

   I. **ENTER ABBREVIATIONS.**
   Enter the abbreviation and what it stands for.

   SG: Swan-Ganz (usually catheter)
   An SG tube was inserted.

   1. _____ (Abbreviation)

   2. _____

   T&A: tonsillectomy and adenoidectomy
   Routine T&A was performed.

   3. _____ (Abbreviation)

   4. _____

   THA: total hip arthroplasty
   He was admitted for revision of right THA.

   5. _____ (Abbreviation)

   6. _____

   TKA: total knee arthroplasty
   He had a TKA performed on the left five years ago.

   7. _____ (Abbreviation)

   8. _____

   TURBT: transurethral resection of the bladder tumor
   He had TURBT performed on the second hospital day.

   9. _____ (Abbreviation)

   10. _____

   TURP: transurethral resection of the prostate
   TURP was performed for BPH.

   11. _____ (Abbreviation)

   12. _____

II. FILL IN THE BLANK.
Use the word(s) above to fill in the blanks.

1. A right total knee _____ was performed for degenerative joint disease.

2. _____ resection of the bladder was carried out.

3. A _____ catheter was inserted via the right IJ approach.

4. Transurethral _____ of the prostate was performed by Urology.

5. A revision total _____ arthroplasty was planned.

6. Tonsillectomy and _____ was performed.

III. FILL IN THE BLANK.
Expand the following abbreviations. For any abbreviation that has more than one expansion, just choose one that is appropriate for this lesson.

1. THA _____   2. TURBT _____

3. SG _____   4. TKA _____

5. TURP _____   6. T&A _____

Review: Surgery

I. **FILL IN THE BLANK.**
   Using the word/word parts in the box, enter the appropriate term in the space provided.

1. Incision and _____

2. Swan-_____ catheter

3. Above-knee _____

4. _____-knee amputation

5. Endo_____

6. _____ blood loss

7. Total knee _____

8. _____ wire

9. _____muscular

10. Intra_____

amputation
arthroplasty
below
drainage
estimated
Ganz
intra
Kirschner
tracheal
venous

II. **MATCHING.**
   Match the word or word part for the appropriate abbreviation expansion. A term may be used more than once.

1. ____ THA – _____ hip arthroplasty

2. ____ TURP – _____ resection of the prostate

3. ____ NG – naso _____ tube

4. ____ T&A – _____ and adenoidectomy

5. ____ ORIF – open _____, internal fixation

6. ____ IM – intra _____

7. ____ I&D – _____ and drainage

8. ____ EGD – esophagogastro _____

9. ____ TURBT – transurethral resection of the bladder _____

10. ____ lap – _____

A. tonsillectomy
B. transurethral
C. duodenoscopy
D. muscular
E. total
F. incision
G. reduction
H. gastric
I. tumor
J. laparotomy

Surgery Abbreviations List

Abbreviation	Expansion
AKA	above-knee amputation
BKA	below-knee amputation
CTR	carpal tunnel release
EBL	estimated blood loss
EGD	esophagogastroduodenoscopy
ET	endotracheal
I&D	incision and drainage
IJ	internal jugular
IM	intramuscular
IV	intravenous
lap	laparotomy/laparoscopic
LR	lactated Ringer's
K-wire	Kirschner wire
NG	nasogastric
ORIF	open reduction, internal fixation
SG	Swan-Ganz
T&A	tonsillectomy and adenoidectomy
THA	total hip arthroplasty
TKA	total knee arthroplasty
TURBT	transurethral resection of bladder tumor
TURP	transurethral resection of prostate

Radiology – Lesson 1

Radiology is much more than simple pictures of bones or of the chest. Although simple radiology studies such as an x-ray of the foot, wrist, or chest are still commonly used, radiology has now expanded to include many complex studies, scans and procedures. The next few lessons will expose you (pun intended) to common abbreviations associated with radiologic studies.

I. ENTER ABBREVIATIONS.
Enter the abbreviation and what it stands for.

AP/PA: anteroposterior/posteroanterior
PA chest was performed.

1. _____ (Abbreviation)

2. _____

BE: barium enema
After GI consult, BE was performed.

3. _____ (Abbreviation)

4. _____

CT: computed tomography
A CT scan of the abdomen and pelvis was carried out.

5. _____ (Abbreviation)

6. _____

EEG: electroencephalogram
As part of her sleep workup an EEG was performed.

7. _____ (Abbreviation)

8. _____

ERCP: endoscopic retrograde cholangiopancreatography
ERCP was performed.

9. _____ (Abbreviation)

10. _____

GI: gastrointestinal
An upper GI with small bowel follow-through was performed.

11. _____ (Abbreviation)

12. _____

Upper GI is the common term for an examination of that area.

II. FILL IN THE BLANK.
Use the word(s) above to fill in the blanks.

1. The chest was photographed in the antero_____ dimension.

2. An electro_____ was performed.

3. An upper _____ exam was normal.

106

4. _____ tomography images were taken of the brain.

5. An endoscopic retrograde _____ was performed.

6. _____ enema was within normal limits.

III. **FILL IN THE BLANK.**
   Expand the following abbreviations. For any abbreviation that has more than one expansion, just choose one that is appropriate for this lesson.

1. ERCP_____   2. BE_____

3. CT_____   4. EEG_____

5. GI_____   6. AP/PA_____

Radiology – Lesson 2

I. **ENTER ABBREVIATIONS.**
   Enter the abbreviation and what it stands for.

HIDA: hydroxyiminodiacetic acid
A HIDA scan was done.

1. _____ (Abbreviation)

2. _____

This is pronounced "hida" (with a long i sound as in "find"). The individual letters are not dictated out.

IVP: intravenous pyelogram
An IVP was entirely within normal limits.

3. _____ (Abbreviation)

4. _____

KUB: kidneys, ureters, bladder (abdominal x-ray)
KUB was performed.

5. _____ (Abbreviation)

6. _____

MRI: magnetic resonance imaging
An MRI of the chest, abdomen, and pelvis was carried out.

7. _____ (Abbreviation)

8. _____

MUGA: multiple gated acquisition
On MUGA images there were no abnormalities.

    9. _____ (Abbreviation)

    10. _____

This is pronounced "mugga," and it is nearly always dictated that way.

OCG: oral cholecystogram
She had an OCG which was negative.

    11. _____ (Abbreviation)

    12. _____

VCUG: voiding cystourethrogram
VCUG showed no abnormalities.

    13. _____ (Abbreviation)

    14. _____

II. FILL IN THE BLANK.
Use the word(s) above to fill in the blanks.

1. A _____ acid scan was performed.

2. _____ pyelogram was ordered.

3. The doctor ordered a _____, ureters, and 4._____ x-ray.

5. Multiple _____ scan was normal.

6. _____ resonance imaging of the brain was performed.

7. An oral _____ was done.

8. Voiding _____ was normal.

III. FILL IN THE BLANK.
Expand the following abbreviations. For any abbreviation that has more than one expansion, just choose one that is appropriate for this lesson.

1. MUGA_____   2. IVP_____

3. MRI_____   4. HIDA_____

5. KUB _____   6. VCUG _____

7. OCG _____

Review: Radiology

I. **FILL IN THE BLANK.**
   Using the word/word parts in the box, enter the appropriate term in the space provided.

1. antero _____

2. _____ cholecystogram

3. multiple _____

4. endoscopic _____

5. upper _____

6. _____ encephalogram

7. kidneys, _____, bladder

8. _____ tomography

9. _____ cystourethrogram

10. _____ resonance 11. _____

12. hydroxy _____ acid

13. intravenous _____

14. barium _____

computed
electro
enema
gastrointestinal
gated acquisition
imaging
iminodiacetic
magnetic
oral
posterior
pyelogram
retrograde cholangiopancreatography
ureters
voiding

II. MULTIPLE CHOICE.
Choose the best answer.

1. EEG
   - ◯ electroechocardiogram
   - ◯ electroencephalography
   - ◯ electroencephalogram
   - ◯ echoenceophalogram

2. BE
   - ◯ barioenema
   - ◯ barium enema
   - ◯ barium encephalogram
   - ◯ bladder electrography

3. PA
   - ◯ proximal anterior
   - ◯ proximoanteral
   - ◯ posterioranterior
   - ◯ posteroanterior

4. IVP
   - ◯ intestinopyelogram
   - ◯ intraventricular pancreatography
   - ◯ intraventricular pyelogram
   - ◯ intravenous pyelogram

5. MRI
   - ◯ magnetic resonance imaging
   - ◯ magnetic rhythm incephalogram
   - ◯ macrorythm imaging
   - ◯ magneticrecognizanceimagery

6. GI
   - ◯ genitointestinal
   - ◯ genitointravenous
   - ◯ gastrointestinal
   - ◯ gastrointestinle

7. CT
   - ◯ computer tomography
   - ◯ computer topography
   - ◯ computed topography
   - ◯ computed tomography

8. KUB
   - ◯ kidneys under bladder
   - ◯ kidneys, urethra, bladder
   - ◯ kidneys, ureters, bladder
   - ◯ kidneys, uvula, bladder

9. OCG
   - ◯ oral cystogram
   - ◯ oral cholangiopancreatography
   - ◯ oral computed gramography
   - ◯ oral cholecystogram

10. MUGA
    - ◯ magnetic upper gaited acquisition
    - ◯ multiple gaited acquisition
    - ◯ multiple gastric acquisition
    - ◯ multiple gated acquisition

Radiology Abbreviations List

Abbreviation	Expansion
PA	posteroanterior
BE	barium enema
CT	computed tomography
EEG	electroencephalogram
ERCP	endoscopic retrograde cholangiopancreatography
GI	gastrointestinal
HIDA	hydroxyiminodiacetic acid
IVP	intravenous pyelogram
KUB	kidneys, ureters, bladder
MRI	magnetic resonance imaging
MUGA	multiple gated acquisition

OCG	oral cholecystogram
VCUG	voiding cystourethrogram

Cardiology – Lesson 1

Cardiology refers to the study and treatment of heart problems. The heart is a complex structure and heart problems often lead to secondary problems and symptoms throughout the body. So cardiology abbreviations show up in all types of reports. Knowing the cardiac basics will be helpful to you, regardless of the kind of coding work you do.

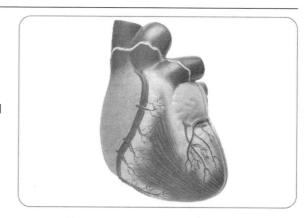

I. **ENTER ABBREVIATIONS.**
   Enter the abbreviation and what it stands for. For any abbreviation that has more than one expansion, just choose one.

A-fib: atrial fibrillation
He went into A-fib.

   1. _____ (Abbreviation)

   2. _____

ASCAD: arteriosclerotic coronary artery disease (atherosclerotic coronary artery disease)
His past medical history is significant for ASCAD.

   3. _____ (Abbreviation)

   4. _____

ACLS: advanced cardiac life support
The patient was given ACLS.

   5. _____ (Abbreviation)

   6. _____

ASCVD: arteriosclerotic cardiovascular disease (atherosclerotic cardiovascular disease)
Cardiac catheterization revealed advanced ASCVD.

   7. _____ (Abbreviation)

   8. _____

ASHD: arteriosclerotic heart disease (atherosclerotic heart disease)
On family history, it was discovered that both the patient's parents died of ASHD.

   9. _____ (Abbreviation)

   10. _____

AV: atrioventricular
AV nodal ablation was performed to correct chronic atrial fibrillation.

11. _____ (Abbreviation)

12. _____

II. FILL IN THE BLANK.
Use the word(s) above to fill in the blanks.

1. She was in atrial _____ on admission.

2. Her _____ coronary artery disease required CABG.

3. She was taken off advanced _____ life support.

4. _____ heart disease is exacerbated by smoking.

5. There was an atrio _____ groove.

6. The patient was 95 years old and had no evidence of atherosclerotic cardio _____

   disease.

III. FILL IN THE BLANK.
Expand the following abbreviations. For any abbreviation that has more than one expansion, just choose one that is appropriate for this lesson.

1. ASCAD_____   2. ASCVD_____

3. AV_____   4. A-fib_____

5. ASHD_____   6. ACLS_____

Cardiology – Lesson 2

I. ENTER ABBREVIATIONS.
Enter the abbreviation and what it stands for.

CABG: coronary artery bypass grafting
He underwent CABG for severe three-vessel disease.

1. _____ (Abbreviation)

2. _____

This abbreviation is often pronounced "cabbage," although it can be C-A-B-G.

ECG/EKG: electrocardiogram (electrocardiography)
His EKG showed an ST depression.

    3. _____ (Abbreviation)

    4. _____

EF: ejection fraction
Her ejection fraction was 23%.

    5. _____ (Abbreviation)

    6. _____

fem-fem: femoral-femoral
The patient had coronary artery bypass graft with fem-fem anastomosis.

    7. _____ (Abbreviation)

    8. _____

fem-pop: femoral-popliteal
A femoral-popliteal bypass was performed due to blockage of the patient's femoral artery.

    9. _____ (Abbreviation)

    10. _____

II. FILL IN THE BLANK.
Use the word(s) or abbreviations above to fill in the blanks.

1. "We then performed the _____ -pop anastomosis."

2. Coronary _____ bypass [3.]_____ times four was planned.

4. There was an _____ fraction of 26%.

5. An _____ gram was performed and was entirely normal.

6. Tissue for the _____ portion of the surgery was taken from the right leg.

III. **FILL IN THE BLANK.**
Expand the following abbreviations. For any abbreviation that has more than one expansion, just choose one that is appropriate for this lesson.

1. EF _____   2. CABG _____

3. fem-fem _____   4. fem-pop _____

5. ECG _____

Cardiology – Lesson 3

I. **ENTER ABBREVIATIONS.**
Enter the abbreviation and what it stands for.

IVC: inferior vena cava
The IVC was spared.

1. _____ (Abbreviation)

2. _____

LAD: left anterior descending (artery)
The LAD was free of disease.

3. _____ (Abbreviation)

4. _____

LAO: left anterior oblique
Films were taken in the LAO projection.

5. _____ (Abbreviation)

6. _____

LCA: left coronary artery (left circumflex artery)
The LCA had a 30% plaque.

7. _____ (Abbreviation)

8. _____

LIMA: left internal mammary artery
Her LIMA was unaffected by disease.

9. _____ (Abbreviation)

10. _____

This is often pronounced "LIMA," with an ee sound for the I.

II. FILL IN THE BLANK.
Use the word(s) above to fill in the blanks.

1. The left _____ descending artery was normal.

2. The _____ internal 3._____ artery
    was free of disease.

4. The _____ vena 5._____ was
    normal.

6. The left anterior _____ position was utilized.

7. The left _____ artery is occluded.

III. FILL IN THE BLANK.
Expand the following abbreviations. For any abbreviation that has more than one expansion, just choose one that is appropriate for this lesson.

1. LCA _____   2. LIMA _____

3. IVC _____   4. LAO _____

5. LAD _____

Cardiology – Lesson 4

I. ENTER ABBREVIATIONS.
Enter the abbreviation and what it stands for.

LV: left ventricle (ventricular)
Normal LV function.

1. _____ (Abbreviation)

2. _____

MI: myocardial infarction
She has a history of MI two years ago.

3. _____ (Abbreviation)

4. _____

OMB: obtuse marginal branch
Her OMB was totally occluded.

5. _____ (Abbreviation)

6. _____

PDA: patent ductus arteriosus (posterior descending artery)
The infant had a PDA.
Evidence of ASCAD was found in the PDA.

    7. _____ (Abbreviation)

    8. _____

    9. _____

PE: pulmonary embolism (embolus)
Ventilation/perfusion scan indicated a possible PE.

    10. _____ (Abbreviation)

    11. _____

PTCA: percutaneous transluminal coronary angioplasty
She presents for cardiac catheterization and probable PTCA.

    12. _____ (Abbreviation)

    13. _____

PVC: premature ventricular contraction
She had persistent PVCs.

    14. _____ (Abbreviation)

    15. _____

PVD: peripheral vascular disease
Coolness of his extremities was consistent with PVD.

    16. _____ (Abbreviation)

    17. _____

II. FILL IN THE BLANK.
Use the word(s) above to fill in the blanks.

    1. She has a history of premature _____.

    2. _____ infarction was ruled out.

    3. She had an occluded _____ marginal branch.

    4. _____ coronary 5._____ was attempted.

    6. She has normal left _____ function.

    7. Given his history, pulmonary _____ was part of the differential diagnosis.

    8. The infant was diagnosed with _____ arteriosus.

9. The PTCA showed 80% occlusion of the posterior _____ artery.

10. _____ vascular disease is the cause of deep venous thrombosis.

III. **FILL IN THE BLANK.**
   Expand the following abbreviations. For any abbreviation that has more than one expansion, just choose one that is appropriate for this lesson.

   1. OMB _____   2. LV _____

   3. PVC _____   4. MI _____

   5. PTCA _____   6. PDA _____

   7. PE _____   8. PVD _____

Cardiology – Lesson 5

I. **ENTER ABBREVIATIONS.**
   Enter the abbreviation and what it stands for.

   RAD: right anterior descending (artery)
   She had a normal RAD.

   1. _____ (Abbreviation)

   2. _____

   RAO: right anterior oblique
   Films were taken in RAO and LAO projections.

   3. _____ (Abbreviation)

   4. _____

   RCA: right coronary artery
   She had a totally occluded RCA.

   5. _____ (Abbreviation)

   6. _____

   Occasionally, this can also be right circumflex artery.

SMA: superior mesenteric artery
His SMA was damaged in the accident.

    7. _____ (Abbreviation)

    8. _____

SMA also has reference to a panel of laboratory tests.

SVC: superior vena cava
His SVC was visualized.

    9. _____ (Abbreviation)

    10. _____

V-tach: ventricular tachycardia
The patient went into acute V-tach.

    11. _____ (Abbreviation)

    12. _____

II. **FILL IN THE BLANK.**
   Use the word(s) above to fill in the blanks.

    1. The right _____ oblique position was used.

    2. The right _____ artery was damaged.

    3. The patient went into _____ tachycardia.

    4. The superior _____ was within normal limits.

    5. Right anterior _____ artery was totally occluded.

    6. Superior _____ artery is found in the abdomen.

III. **FILL IN THE BLANK.**
   Expand the following abbreviations. For any abbreviation that has more than one expansion, just choose one that is appropriate for this lesson.

1. V-tach _____   2. SVC _____

3. RAD _____   4. RCA _____

5. RAO _____   6. SMA _____

Review: Cardiology

I. FILL IN THE BLANK.
Using the word/word parts in the box, enter the appropriate term in the space provided.

1. premature _____ contractions

2. ventricular _____

3. right _____ oblique

4. inferior _____ cava

5. patent ductus _____

6. left anterior _____

7. peripheral _____ disease

8. left internal _____ artery

9. _____ vena cava

10. _____ infarction

anterior
arteriosus
descending
mammary
myocardial
superior
tachycardia
vascular
vena
ventricular

II. MATCHING.
Match the word or word part to the abbreviation expansion.

1. ____ V-tach – _____ tachycardia

2. ____ CABG – coronary artery bypass _____

3. ____ PTCA – percutaneous _____ coronary angioplasty

4. ____ EF – _____ fraction

5. ____ LCA – left _____ artery

6. ____ PE – pulmonary _____

7. ____ SMA – superior _____ artery

8. ____ RAO – right anterior _____

9. ____ ASHD – _____ heart disease

10. ____ LCA – _____ coronary artery

A. ejection
B. oblique
C. ventricular
D. grafting
E. embolism
F. mesenteric
G. left
H. transluminal
I. atherosclerotic
J. circumflex

III. MULTIPLE CHOICE.
Choose the best answer.

1. LV
   - ○ leftover ventricle
   - ○ lead ventricle
   - ○ left ventricle
   - ○ left ventrical

2. OMB
   - ○ obtuse marginal branch
   - ○ outer marginal branch
   - ○ obtuse main branch
   - ○ outer margin brachial

3. PDA
   - ○ patient ductus arteriosus
   - ○ patent ductis artiosis
   - ○ patent ductus arteriosis
   - ○ patent ductus arteriosus

4. PVD
   - ○ premature ventricular disease
   - ○ peripheral vascular disease
   - ○ peripheral ventricular disease
   - ○ premature vascular disease

5. fem-pop
   - ○ femoral-popliteal
   - ○ femoral-poplitial
   - ○ female-poplitial
   - ○ femoral-popaliteal

6. ASCAD
   - ○ arteriosclerotic cardiac anginal disease
   - ○ artriosclerotic coronary artery disease
   - ○ arteriosclerotic coronary artery disease
   - ○ arteriosclerotic cardiovascular artery disease

7. A-fib

○ anterior fibula
○ anterior fibrillation
○ atrial fibrilation
○ atrial fibrillation

8. ACLS

○ advanced coronary living support
○ advanced cardiac life support
○ atherosclerotic coronary life support
○ arteriosclerotic cardiovascular life support

9. IVC

○ inferior venous cardiography
○ inferior venous cava
○ inferior vena cava
○ inner vena cava

10. MI

○ myocardial infarction
○ mycardial infarction
○ myocardial infraction
○ myocardile infarction

Cardiology Abbreviations List

Abbreviation	Expansion
AF	atrial fibrillation
ASCAD	arteriosclerotic coronary artery disease/atherosclerotic coronary artery disease
ACLS	advanced cardiac life support
ASCVD	arteriosclerotic cardiovascular disease/atherosclerotic cardiovascular disease
ASHD	arteriosclerotic heart disease/atherosclerotic heart disease
AV	atrioventricular
CABG	coronary artery bypass grafting/coronary artery bypass graft
ECG/EKG	electrocardiogram/electrocardiography
EF	ejection fraction
fem-fem	femoral-femoral
fem-pop	femoral-popliteal
IVC	inferior vena cava

LAD	left anterior descending
LAO	left anterior oblique
LCA	left coronary artery/left circumflex artery
LIMA	left internal mammary artery
LV	left ventricle
MI	myocardial infarction
OMB	obtuse marginal branch
PDA	patent ductus arteriosus/posterior descending artery
PE	pulmonary embolism
PTCA	percutaneous transluminal coronary angioplasty
PVC	premature ventricular contraction
PVD	peripheral vascular disease
RAD	right anterior descending
RAO	right anterior oblique
RCA	right coronary artery
SMA	superior mesenteric artery
SVC	superior vena cava
V-tach	ventricular tachycardia

Fetal Measurements – Lesson 1

Obstetrics and Gynecology is a field that frequently uses abbreviations. They are used especially for terms related to pregnancy and delivery. The following are abbreviated terms that you will see often in all kinds of OB/GYN reports, as well as in reports containing a history and physical (H&P) examination for female patients.

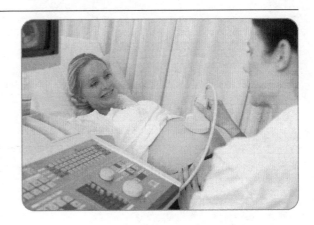

I. **ENTER ABBREVIATIONS.**
   Enter the abbreviation and what it stands for.

   AC: abdominal circumference

   1. _____ (Abbreviation)

   2. _____

BPD: biparietal diameter

   3. _____ (Abbreviation)

   4. _____

EFW: estimated fetal weight

   5. _____ (Abbreviation)

   6. _____

FL: femur length

   7. _____ (Abbreviation)

   8. _____

HC: head circumference

   9. _____ (Abbreviation)

   10. _____

MEASUREMENTS: BPD 8.3 cm for 32.1 weeks, HC 11.0 cm for 32.6 weeks, AC 14.2 cm for 33.1 weeks, and FL 4.5 cm for 32.8 weeks.

II. **FILL IN THE BLANK.**
Expand the following abbreviations. For any abbreviation that has more than one expansion, just choose one appropriate for this lesson.

1. BPD_____   2. FL_____

3. EFW_____   4. AC_____

5. HC_____

General History – Lesson 2

I. **ENTER ABBREVIATIONS.**
Enter the abbreviation and what it stands for.

AB: abortion or abortus
(can also be written "ab")

   1. _____ (Abbreviation)

   2. _____

G: gravida (# of pregnancies)

   3. _____ (Abbreviation)

   4. _____

P: para (# of living children)

    5. _____ (Abbreviation)

    6. _____

SAB: spontaneous abortion

    7. _____ (Abbreviation)

    8. _____

TAB: therapeutic abortion

    9. _____ (Abbreviation)

    10. _____

The patient is a G5, P3, AB2 (SAB 1, TAB 1).

II. FILL IN THE BLANK.
Expand the following abbreviations. For any abbreviation that has more than one expansion, just choose one appropriate for this lesson.

1. G _____   2. AB _____

3. SAB _____   4. P _____

5. TAB _____

Obstetrical Terms – Lesson 3

I. ENTER ABBREVIATIONS.
Enter the abbreviation and what it stands for.

C-section: cesarean section
The patient has a history of C-section times two in the past.

    1. _____ (Abbreviation)

    2. _____

CPD: cephalopelvic disproportion
C-section was performed secondary to CPD.

    3. _____ (Abbreviation)

    4. _____

EDC: estimated date of confinement
She has a gestational age of 26.4 weeks, giving her an EDC of 2-12-94.

    5. _____ (Abbreviation)

    6. _____

EGA: estimated gestational age
The patient has an EGA of 32.9 weeks.

    7. _____ (Abbreviation)

    8. _____

IUGR: intrauterine growth retardation
There is evidence of IUGR.

    9. _____ (Abbreviation)

    10. _____

II. FILL IN THE BLANK.
Use the word(s) above to fill in the blanks.

    1. She underwent elective _____ section without complications.

    2. Ultrasound dates gave her an estimated date of _____ of 13 April 91.

    3. She should return for a followup ultrasound because of _____ growth
       4. _____.

    5. She underwent pelvimetry for possible _____ disproportion.

    6. She has an _____ gestational age of 22.4 weeks.

Obstetrical Terms – Lesson 4

I. ENTER ABBREVIATIONS.
Enter the abbreviation and what it stands for.

L&D: labor and delivery
The patient was taken to L&D and delivered triplets.

    1. _____ (Abbreviation)

    2. _____

LGA: large for gestational age
The fetus shows an LGA growth curve.

    3. _____ (Abbreviation)

    4. _____

LMP: last menstrual period
Her LMP is 18 June, giving her an EDC of 28 March.

    5. _____ (Abbreviation)

    6. _____

MSAFP: maternal serum alpha fetoprotein
She is MSAFP negative.

    7. _____ (Abbreviation)

    8. _____

NSVD: normal spontaneous vaginal delivery
She was admitted and had an NSVD.

    9. _____ (Abbreviation)

    10. _____

ROM: rupture of membranes
She had spontaneous ROM before coming to the hospital.

    11. _____ (Abbreviation)

    12. _____

VBAC: vaginal birth after cesarean (Usually pronounced V-back)
The patient wished to attempt VBAC.

    13. _____ (Abbreviation)

    14. _____

II. FILL IN THE BLANK.
Use the word(s) above to fill in the blanks.

    1. Her last _____ period was in 1978.

    2. She had normal _____ vaginal delivery.

    3. She was large for a _____ age baby.

    4. Maternal serum _____ was normal.

    5. _____ after cesarean was attempted.

    6. She presented to the ER with _____ of membranes.

    7. She was in labor and _____ for 36 hours.

III. FILL IN THE BLANK.
Expand the following abbreviations. For any abbreviation that has more than one expansion, just choose one appropriate for this lesson.

1. LGA _____

2. C-section _____

3. LMP _____

4. CPD _____

5. MSAFP _____

6. IUGR _____

7. EDC _____

8. EGA _____

9. ROM _____

10. NSVD _____

11. VBAC _____

12. L&D _____

Gynecology Terms – Lesson 5

I. ENTER ABBREVIATIONS.
Enter the abbreviation and what it stands for.

BSO: bilateral salpingo-oophorectomy
She underwent TAH-BSO in 1974.

1. _____ (Abbreviation)

2. _____

D&C: dilatation and curettage (dilation and curettage)
She had a D&C as treatment for intermenstrual bleeding.

3. _____ (Abbreviation)

4. _____

PID: pelvic inflammatory disease
She was sent to the emergency room for possible PID.

5. _____ (Abbreviation)

6. _____

TAH: total abdominal hysterectomy (often TAH-BSO)
She had a TAH performed immediately following cesarean section.

7. _____ (Abbreviation)

8. _____

TVH: total vaginal hysterectomy
She presents for TVH.

9. _____ (Abbreviation)

10. _____

II. FILL IN THE BLANK.
Use the word(s) above to fill in the blanks.

1. She is having infertility problems secondary to a history of pelvic _____ disease.

2. Bilateral _____-oophorectomy was performed secondary to a cystic mass on the left ovary.

3. Total abdominal _____ was performed.

4. Total _____ hysterectomy was performed.

5. Dilatation and _____ was indicated for hypermenorrhea.

III. FILL IN THE BLANK.
Expand the following abbreviations. For any abbreviation that has more than one expansion, just choose one appropriate for this lesson.

1. TAH-BSO _____

2. TVH _____

3. D&C _____

4. PID _____

5. BSO _____

Review: Obstetrics and Gynecology

I. FILL IN THE BLANK.
Some spaces may require more than one word. Be sure to provide the complete answer. For any question that may have more than one appropriate answer, just choose one.

1. abdominal _____

2. cephalopelvic _____

3. pelvic _____ disease

4. spontaneous _____

5. _____ date of confinement

6. last menstrual _____

7. intrauterine _____ retardation

8. total abdominal _____

9. _____ length

10. bilateral salpingo-_____

abortion
circumference
disproportion
estimated
femur
growth
hysterectomy
inflammatory
oophorectomy
period

II. MULTIPLE CHOICE.
Choose the correct word or word part for the abbreviation expansion.

1. CPD – (◯ craniopelvic, ◯ cephalopelvic) disproportion

2. TAB – (◯ therapeutic, ◯ total) abortion

3. AC – (◯ amniotic, ◯ abdominal) circumference

4. EDC – estimated date of (◯ cesarean, ◯ confinement)

5. LGA – large for (◯ gestational, ◯ genetic) age

6. VBAC – vaginal birth after (◯ cesarean, ◯ confinement)

7. MSAFP – maternal serum (◯ after, ◯ alpha) fetoprotein

8. FL – (◯ femur, ◯ fetal) length

9. EFW – (◯ exact, ◯ estimated) fetal weight

10. HC – (◯ head, ◯ heart) circumference

III. MATCHING.
Match the word or word part to the abbreviation expansion.

1. ____ SAB – _____ abortion
2. ____ G – _____
3. ____ BPD – biparietal _____
4. ____ ROM – rupture of _____
5. ____ D&C – _____ and curettage
6. ____ P – _____
7. ____ TVH – total _____ hysterectomy
8. ____ PID – pelvic _____ disease
9. ____ L&D – labor and _____
10. ____ IUGR – _____ growth retardation

A. diameter
B. membrane
C. gravida
D. spontaneous
E. intrauterine
F. dilatation
G. delivery
H. vaginal
I. para
J. inflammatory

Obstetrics and Gynecology Abbreviations List

Abbreviation	Expansion
AC	abdominal circumference
BPD	biparietal diameter
EFW	estimated fetal weight
FL	femur length
HC	head circumference
AB	abortion
G	gravida
P	para
SAB	spontaneous abortion
TAB	therapeutic abortion
TPAL	**t**erm infants, **p**remature infants, **a**bortions, **l**iving children
C-section	cesarean section
CPD	cephalopelvic disproportion
EDC	estimated date of confinement
EGA	estimated gestational age
IUGR	intrauterine growth retardation
L&D	labor and delivery
LGA	large for gestational age
LMP	last menstrual period

MSAFP	maternal serum alpha fetoprotein
NSVD	normal spontaneous vaginal delivery
ROM	rupture of membranes
VBAC	vaginal birth after cesarean
BSO	bilateral salpingo-oophorectomy
D&C	dilation and curettage
PID	pelvic inflammatory disease
TAH	total abdominal hysterectomy
TVH	total vaginal hysterectomy

Orthopedics – Lesson 1

Orthopedics is a branch of medicine concerned with the skeletal system, its articulations and associated structures. The following are abbreviations related to bones, joints, and associated ligaments. There are now many more orthopedic surgical procedures being performed than in the past. This requires the medical coder to know the meanings of these abbreviations so they may accurately code the operations and procedures.

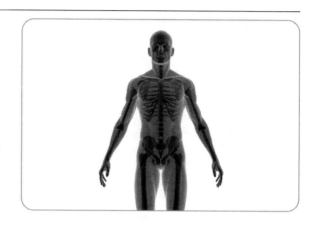

I. **ENTER ABBREVIATIONS.**
   Enter the abbreviation and what it stands for.

   AC: acromioclavicular
   The AC joint is intact.

   1. _____ (Abbreviation)

   2. _____

   ACL: anterior cruciate ligament
   There is evidence of a torn ACL.

   3. _____ (Abbreviation)

   4. _____

   AFO: ankle-foot orthosis (ankle-foot orthotic)
   He required AFO for his malleolar deformity.

   5. _____ (Abbreviation)

   6. _____

C-spine: cervical spine
The C-spine was imaged.

    7. _____ (Abbreviation)

    8. _____

CMC: carpometacarpal (joint)
The CMC is normal.

    9. _____ (Abbreviation)

    10. _____

DDD: degenerative disc disease or degenerative disk disease (with a k)
Spinal x-rays revealed DDD.

    11. _____ (Abbreviation)

    12. _____

DIP: distal interphalangeal (joint)
There is no DIP separation.

    13. _____ (Abbreviation)

    14. _____

II. FILL IN THE BLANK.
Use the word(s) above to fill in the blanks.

1. The acromio _____ joint is separated.

2. There is no anterior _____ ligament instability.

3. The _____ spine is within normal limits.

4. The _____ metacarpal is normal.

5. The distal _____ joint is intact.

6. His ankle-foot _____ helped to alleviate the problem.

7. His _____ disc disease caused him great pain.

III. **FILL IN THE BLANK.**
   Expand the following abbreviations. For any abbreviation that has more than one expansion, just choose one that is appropriate for this lesson.

1. DIP_____   2. AC_____

3. CMC_____   4. C-spine_____

5. ACL_____   6. AFO_____

7. DDD_____

Orthopedics – Lesson 2

I. **ENTER ABBREVIATIONS.**
   Enter the abbreviation and what it stands for.

IP: interphalangeal
The IP joint is intact.

1. _____ (Abbreviation)

2. _____

IT: iliotibial
The iliotibial band is visualized and is within normal limits.

3. _____ (Abbreviation)

4. _____

L-spine: lumbar spine
A lumbar spine film was done.

5. _____ (Abbreviation)

6. _____

LS: lumbosacral (spine)
The lumbosacral spine film is normal.

7. _____ (Abbreviation)

8. _____

MCL: medial collateral ligament
He injured his MCL playing football.

9. _____ (Abbreviation)

10. _____

MCP: metacarpophalangeal (joint)
The MCP joint is unremarkable.

11. _____ (Abbreviation)

12. _____

II. FILL IN THE BLANK.
Use the word(s) above to fill in the blanks.

1. The _____ band is intact.

2. The _____ phalangeal joint is unremarkable.

3. Lumbo _____ spine is within normal limits.

4. The right inter _____ joint was visualized.

5. There is slight straightening of the _____ spine.

6. Medial _____ ligament was assessed by arthroscopy.

III. FILL IN THE BLANK.
Expand the following abbreviations. For any abbreviation that has more than one expansion, just choose one that is appropriate for this lesson.

1. MCP_____   2. L-spine_____

3. IP_____   4. LS_____

5. IT_____   6. MCL_____

Orthopedics – Lesson 3

I. ENTER ABBREVIATIONS.
Enter the abbreviation and what it stands for.

MTP: metatarsophalangeal (joint)
The MTP joint is normal.

1. _____ (Abbreviation)

2. _____

PCL: posterior cruciate ligament
No laxity of the PCL.

3. _____ (Abbreviation)

4. _____

PIP: proximal interphalangeal
The PIP joint is unremarkable.

    5. _____ (Abbreviation)

    6. _____

SI: sacroiliac (joint)
The SI joints were scanned and were within normal limits.

    7. _____ (Abbreviation)

    8. _____

T-spine: thoracic spine
The thoracic spine was imaged from T1–T12.

    9. _____ (Abbreviation)

    10. _____

tib-fib: tibial-fibular or tibiofibular
X-ray showed a right tib-fib fracture.

    11. _____ (Abbreviation)

    12. _____

The abbreviation tib-fib is nearly always used as an adjective. Occasionally, however, it is used as a noun (tibia-fibula).

TMJ: temporomandibular joint
The TMJ moved normally.

    13. _____ (Abbreviation)

    14. _____

II. FILL IN THE BLANK.
Use the word(s) above to fill in the blanks.

    1. The _____ cruciate ligament is intact.

    2. The _____ mandibular joint is imaged.

    3. _____ iliac joints appear intact.

    4. AP and lateral views of the _____ spine were obtained.

    5. The _____ interphalangeal joint appears intact.

    6. On views of the right foot, the _____ phalangeal joint was noted to be separated.

    7. The tibial-_____ fracture was casted.

III. **FILL IN THE BLANK.**
   Expand the following abbreviations. For any abbreviation that has more than one expansion, just choose one that is appropriate for this lesson.

1. MTP_____   2. SI_____

3. T-spine_____   4. TMJ_____

5. PCL_____   6. PIP_____

7. tib-fib_____

Review: Orthopedics

I. **FILL IN THE BLANK.**
   Using the word/word parts in the box, enter the appropriate term in the space provided.

1. tibial-_____

2. acromio_____

3. degenerative_____ disease

4. lumbo_____

5. _____carpal

6. ilio_____

7. medial_____ ligament

8. ankle-foot_____

9. posterior_____ ligament

10. distal_____

carpometa
clavicular
collateral
cruciate
disc
fibular
interphalangeal
orthosis
sacral
tibial

II. MATCHING.
Match the word or word part for the appropriate abbreviation expansion. A term may be used more than once.

1. ____ SI – _____ iliac
2. ____ MCP – metacarpo _____
3. ____ TMJ – _____ joint
4. ____ L-spine – _____ spine
5. ____ IP – inter _____
6. ____ ACL – anterior _____
7. ____ PIP – proximal _____
8. ____ C-spine – _____ spine
9. ____ MTP – metatarso _____
10. ____ T-spine – _____ spine

A. temporomandibular
B. cruciate ligament
C. phalangeal
D. sacro
E. meta
F. cervical
G. lumbar
H. interphalangeal
I. thoracic

III. MULTIPLE CHOICE.
Choose the best answer.

1. AFO
   - ○ ankle for orthosis
   - ○ another foot orthopedic
   - ○ ankle-foot orthosis
   - ○ ankle-foot orthopedic

2. DIP
   - ○ dorsal interphalangeal
   - ○ distal interphalangeal
   - ○ distal innerphalangeal
   - ○ dorsum innerspace proximal

3. LS
   - ○ lumbosacral
   - ○ lumbasacrol
   - ○ lumbasacral
   - ○ lumbosacrol

4. AC

○ acromoclavicular
○ aceromyoclavicular
○ acromioclavicular
○ acromyoclaviculer

5. DDD

○ disc disease degeneration
○ degenerating disease of the discs
○ disco degeneration disease
○ degenerative disc disease

6. PCL

○ posterior cruciate ligament
○ proximal cruciate ligament
○ proximal clavicular ligament
○ posterior clavicular ligament

7. IT

○ interotibial
○ innertibial
○ iliotibial
○ ileotibial

8. TMJ

○ temporamandible joint
○ temporomandicular joint
○ temporomandibular joint
○ temperomandibular joint

9. PIP

○ posterior innerphalangeal
○ posterior interphalangeal
○ proximal innerphalangeal
○ proximal interphalangeal

10. CMC

○ carpometacruciate
○ carpometacarpal
○ claviculometacarpal
○ claviculometaclavicular

Orthopedics Abbreviations List

Abbreviation	Expansion
AC	acromioclavicular
ACL	anterior cruciate ligament
AFO	ankle-foot orthosis (ankle-foot orthotic)
C-spine	cervical spine
CMC	carpometacarpal
DDD	degenerative disc disease or degenerative disk disease
DIP	distal interphalangeal (joint)
IT	iliotibial
L-spine	lumbar spine
LS	lumbosacral (spine)
MCL	medial collateral ligament
MCP	metacarpophalangeal (joint)
MTP	metatarsophalangeal (joint)
PCL	posterior cruciate ligament
PIP	proximal interphalangeal
SI	sacroiliac (joint)
T-spine	thoracic spine
tib-fib	tibial-fibular or tibiofibular
TMJ	temporomandibular joint

Miscellaneous Abbreviations – Lesson 1

You've made it this far! Do you feel like you are thinking in short forms and abbreviations? Just a few more in the "miscellaneous" category, and you will complete your basic medical terminology training. The last section is a mish-mash of general and specialty abbreviations commonly seen in medical reports. You will notice some terms obviously have reference to specific specialties, but they have been included here in the miscellaneous category because it is not possible for us to cover abbreviations for all the various medical and surgical subspecialties in this unit. Take a deep breath; you are headed for the terminology finish line.

I. **ENTER ABBREVIATIONS.**
   Enter the abbreviation and what it stands for.

   ADA: American Dietetic Association
   The patient was discharged on ADA diet.

   1. _____ (Abbreviation)

   2. _____

ADL: activities of daily living
The patient presents to physical therapy having problems with ADLs.

   3. _____ (Abbreviation)

   4. _____

AMA: against medical advice
The patient signed out AMA.

   5. _____ (Abbreviation)

   6. _____

Note: AMA also means American Medical Association. The context of the report should make this distinction fairly easy.

ASA: acetylsalicylic acid (aspirin)
He was to take ASA daily for his CAD.

   7. _____ (Abbreviation)

   8. _____

AVM: arteriovenous malformation
Head CT showed an AVM.

   9. _____ (Abbreviation)

  10. _____

CLL: chronic lymphocytic leukemia
The primary diagnosis was CLL.

  11. _____ (Abbreviation)

  12. _____

CPAP: continuous positive airway pressure
He was put on CPAP for his sleep apnea.

  13. _____ (Abbreviation)

  14. _____

CPR: cardiopulmonary resuscitation
CPR attempts failed, and the patient was pronounced dead.

  15. _____ (Abbreviation)

  16. _____

II. FILL IN THE BLANK.
Use the word(s) above to fill in the blanks.

1. The patient left the hospital _____ medical
   2. _____.

3. Diet: low-salt, low-fat American _____ Association
   diet.

4. He should be able to resume _____ of daily living.

5. _____ malformation was noted.

6. _____ resuscitation attempts failed.

7. The prognosis for his chronic _____ leukemia was
   poor.

8. The patient could not take _____ acid because of
   gastrointestinal problems.

9. The continuous _____ pressure helped alleviate
   his snoring.

III. FILL IN THE BLANK.
Expand the following abbreviations. For any abbreviation that has more than one expansion, just choose one that is appropriate for this lesson.

1. AMA _____   2. CPR _____

3. ADA _____   4. AVM _____

5. ADL _____   6. ASA _____

7. CLL _____

Miscellaneous Abbreviations – Lesson 2

I. ENTER ABBREVIATIONS.
Enter the abbreviation and what it stands for.

DC: discontinue or discharge
The patient was to DC his medications.
The patient was DC'd after 10 days.

1. _____ (Abbreviation)

2. _____

DNR: DO NOT RESUSCITATE
The patient was counseled and DNR status was confirmed.

3. _____ (Abbreviation)

4. _____

Note that the entire phrase is capitalized. Unless client instructs you otherwise, always type it in caps.

DT: delirium tremens
DTs were noted on presentation at the ER.

5. _____ (Abbreviation)

6. _____

DOB: date of birth
They couldn't find her DOB on her patient chart.

7. _____ (Abbreviation)

8. _____

ESWL: extracorporeal shock-wave lithotripsy
We attempted to destroy the kidney stones with ESWL.

9. _____ (Abbreviation)

10. _____

II. FILL IN THE BLANK.
Use the word(s) above to fill in the blanks.

1. With _____ shock-wave 2._____

   stones can be removed without surgery.

3. Upon admission her chronic medications were

   _____.

4. She is a DO NOT _____ status.

5. Her date of _____ is not recorded on the chart.

6. In spite of a long history of alcoholism, he had no record of

   _____ tremens or blackouts.

III. **FILL IN THE BLANK.**
Expand the following abbreviations. For any abbreviation that has more than one expansion, just choose one that is appropriate for this lesson.

1. DT _____   2. DNR _____

3. DC _____   4. DOB _____

5. ESWL _____

Miscellaneous Abbreviations – Lesson 3

I. **ENTER ABBREVIATIONS.**
Enter the abbreviation and what it stands for.

GE: gastroesophageal
GE reflux is also called heartburn.

1. _____ (Abbreviation)

2. _____

HCTZ: hydrochlorothiazide
HCTZ was part of his high blood pressure control regimen.

3. _____ (Abbreviation)

4. _____

H&P: history and physical
H&P was recorded in the chart.

5. _____ (Abbreviation)

6. _____

HPI: history of present illness
For review of systems, see HPI.

7. _____ (Abbreviation)

8. _____

II. FILL IN THE BLANK.
Use the word(s) above to fill in the blanks.

1. _____ of present illness as noted above.

2. There was ulceration at the _____ junction.

3. _____ has significant side effects in a very few

    patients.

4. History and _____ were absent from the chart.

III. FILL IN THE BLANK.
Expand the following abbreviations. For any abbreviation that has more than one expansion, just choose one that is appropriate for this lesson.

1. HPI _____   2. GE _____

3. HCTZ _____   4. H&P _____

Miscellaneous Abbreviations – Lesson 4

I. ENTER ABBREVIATIONS.
Enter the abbreviation and what it stands for.

IOL: intraocular lens
He had an IOL implant O.D. for cataracts.

1. _____ (Abbreviation)

2. _____

ITP: idiopathic thrombocytopenic purpura
ITP is characterized by small hemorrhages which may be macular or papular.

3. _____ (Abbreviation)

4. _____

LLL: left lower lobe
The patient has LLL pneumonia.

5. _____ (Abbreviation)

6. _____

LOC: loss of consciousness
Despite head trauma, there was no LOC.

7. _____ (Abbreviation)

8. _____

MDI: metered dose inhaler
The patient was given an Albuterol MDI.

9. _____ (Abbreviation)

10. _____

NKDA: no known drug allergies
Allergies: NKDA.

11. _____ (Abbreviation)

12. _____

II. FILL IN THE BLANK.
Use the word(s) above to fill in the blanks.

1. She was given an Atrovent metered _____.

2. Idiopathic _____ purpura has such symptoms as

   easy bruisability.

3. _____ allergies.

4. Loss of _____ was less than one minute.

5. She was admitted for left _____ pneumonia.

6. The _____ lens implant greatly increased her

   visual acuity in the right eye.

III. FILL IN THE BLANK.
Expand the following abbreviations. For any abbreviation that has more than one expansion, just choose one that is appropriate for this lesson.

1. LOC _____   2. IOL _____

3. NKDA _____   4. LLL _____

5. MDI _____   6. ITP _____

I. ENTER ABBREVIATIONS.
Enter the abbreviation and what it stands for.

NPO: nothing by mouth
(NPO is derived from the Latin nil per os.)
She remained NPO on the second postoperative day.

1. _____ (Abbreviation)

2. _____

Can also be written n.p.o. or npo.

Phen-fen: phentermine and fenfluramine
Phen-fen is largely discredited as a weight loss regimen.

3. _____ (Abbreviation)

4. _____

The FDA requested the removal of Phen-fen from the market in 1997. This is also acceptably referred to as fen-phen or Fen-phen. There is acceptable variation to how it is presented.

PND: paroxysmal nocturnal dyspnea
No PND or orthopnea.

5. _____ (Abbreviation)

6. _____

subq: subcutaneous (subcutaneously)
She was injected subq.

7. _____ (Abbreviation)

8. _____

Pronounced sub-Q. Sometimes written subcu.

SOB: shortness of breath
She had severe SOB and was referred to the ER.

9. _____ (Abbreviation)

10. _____

TPN: total parenteral nutrition
She was started on TPN while in the hospital.

11. _____ (Abbreviation)

12. _____

II. FILL IN THE BLANK.
Use the word(s) above to fill in the blanks.

1. She was injected _____.

2. Total _____ nutrition was begun.

3. She had severe _____ of breath.

4. _____ by mouth for two days.

5. No evidence of _____ nocturnal 6._____.

7. The patient developed severe heart disease as a result of taking phentermine and

   _____.

III. FILL IN THE BLANK.
Expand the following abbreviations. For any abbreviation that has more than one expansion, just choose one that is appropriate for this lesson.

1. NPO _____   2. SOB _____

3. TPN _____   4. subq _____

5. PND _____   6. Phen-fen _____

Review: Miscellaneous Abbreviations

I. FILL IN THE BLANK.
Using the word/word parts in the box, enter the appropriate term in the space provided.

1. against medical _____

2. _____ dose inhaler

3. date of _____

4. total _____

5. _____ of daily living

6. _____ lobe

7. loss of _____

8. _____ of breath

9. cardiopulmonary _____

10. dis_____

activities
advice
birth
consciousness
continue
left lower
metered
parenteral nutrition
resuscitation
shortness

II. MATCHING.
Match the word or word part for the appropriate abbreviation expansion. A term may be used more than once.

1. ____ PND – _____ nocturnal dyspnea

2. ____ NKDA – no known drug _____

3. ____ DT – delirium _____

4. ____ CPAP – continuous positive _____ pressure

5. ____ CLL – chronic _____ leukemia

6. ____ ESWL – _____ shock-wave lithotripsy

7. ____ HCTZ – hydro _____

8. ____ HPI – history of present _____

9. ____ ASA – _____ acid

10. ____ IOL – intra _____ lens

A. lymphocytic
B. tremens
C. airway
D. acetylsalicylic
E. paroxysmal
F. chlorothiazide
G. ocular
H. extracorporeal
I. illness
J. allergies

III. MULTIPLE CHOICE.
Choose the correct word or word part for the abbreviation expansion.

1. ADA – American (◯Diabetic, ◯Dietetic) Association

2. AVM – (◯arteriovenous, ◯arterovenous) malformation

3. ITP – idiopathic thrombocytopenic (◯purpura, ◯purpera)

4. CLL – chronic (◯lymphoma, ◯lymphocytic) leukemia

5. SOB – shortness of (◯breadth, ◯breath)

6. MDI – (◯measured, ◯metered) dose inhaler

7. ADL – activities of daily (◯living, ◯life)

8. DC – (◯discontinue, ◯deliriocremens) .

9. LLL – left lower (◯lobe, ◯lung) .

10. TPN – total (◯parental, ◯parenteral) nutrition

Miscellaneous Abbreviations List

Abbreviation	Expansion
ADA	American Dietetic Association
ADL	activites of daily living
AMA	against medical advice
ASA	acetylsalicylic acid
AVM	arteriovenous malformation
CLL	chronic lymphocytic leukemia
CPAP	continuous positive airway pressure
CPR	cardiopulmonary resuscitation
DC	discontinue/discharge
DNR	DO NOT RESUSCITATE
DT	delirium tremens
DOB	date of birth
ESWL	extracorporeal shock-wave lithotripsy
GE	gastroesophageal
HCTZ	hydrochlorothiazide

H&P	history and physical
HPI	history of present illness
IOL	intraocular lens
ITP	idiopathic thrombocytopenic purpura
LLL	left lower lobe
LOC	loss of consciousness
MDI	metered dose inhaler
NKDA	no known drug allergies
NPO	nothing by mouth
PND	paroxysmal nocturnal dyspnea
sub q	subcutaneous
SOB	shortness of breath
TPN	total parenteral nutrition

Answer Key

Plurals

Plurals – Rules 1-3

I. FILL IN THE BLANK.

1. searches
2. histories
3. avulsions
4. extremities
5. calcifications
6. churches
7. cytologies
8. days
9. emergencies
10. fractures
11. duties
12. traumas
13. bosses
14. blushes
15. angiographies
16. echoes
17. leukocytes
18. stitches
19. peduncles
20. theologies

Plurals – Rule 4

I. FILL IN THE BLANK.

1. acetabula
2. antra
3. brachia
4. capitula
5. cava
6. cilia
7. coccidia
8. crania
9. diverticula
10. dorsa
11. endometria
12. endothelia
13. epithelia
14. frenula
15. haustra
16. hila
17. infundibula
18. ischia
19. labia
20. labra
21. mediastina
22. omenta
23. ostia
24. plana
25. pudenda
26. retinacula
27. rostra
28. spatia
29. spectra
30. specula
31. strata
32. tegmenta
33. tentoria
34. tubercula
35. reticula

Plurals – Rule 5

I. FILL IN THE BLANK.

1. adnexa
2. uvulae
3. fasciae
4. stomata
5. trochleae
6. vaginae
7. medullae
8. vertebrae
9. condylomata
10. petechiae
11. valleculae
12. ampullae
13. synechiae
14. plicae
15. portae
16. leiomyomata
17. striae
18. linguae

19. genitalia
21. bullae
23. areolae
25. sellae
27. vesiculae
29. conchae

20. sequelae
22. scatomata
24. conjunctivae
26. stromata
28. aurae
30. sclerae

Plurals – Rule 6

I. FILL IN THE BLANK.

1. stimuli
3. annuli
5. malleoli
7. meatus
9. humeri
11. crura
13. globi
15. vagi
17. corpora
19. thrombi
21. nevi
23. plexus
25. calculi
27. bacilli
29. villi

2. alveoli
4. viscera
6. rami
8. trunci
10. panniculi
12. glomeruli
14. limbi
16. uteri
18. menisci
20. fundi
22. canaliculi
24. bronchi
26. sulci
28. tali
30. tophi

Plurals – Rules 7-8

I. FILL IN THE BLANK.

1. ankyloses
3. irides
5. epiphyses
7. arthritides
9. pubes
11. diaphyses
13. cuspides
15. aponeuroses

2. testes
4. paralyses
6. diureses
8. prostheses
10. anastomoses
12. metastases
14. synchondroses

Plurals – Rule 9

I. FILL IN THE BLANK.

1. appendices
3. cruces
5. calices
7. indices
9. apices
11. cicatrices
13. varices
15. vertices

2. vortices
4. larynges
6. thoraces
8. falces
10. matrices
12. phalanges
14. cervices

Review: Plurals

I. FILL IN THE BLANK.

1. bronchi
2. echoes
3. labra
4. tori
5. adnexa
6. lamellae
7. appendices
8. viscera
9. branches
10. reticula
11. corpora
12. tegmenta
13. mammae
14. condylomata
15. chemistries
16. fistulae
17. falces
18. arthritides
19. panniculi
20. cicatrices
21. metaphyses
22. maxillae
23. meatus
24. foramina
25. specula
26. irides
27. humeri
28. cervices
29. lumina
30. spectra
31. apophyses
32. sulci
33. phalanges
34. malleoli
35. pelves
36. rami
37. plexus
38. synechiae
39. prostheses
40. babies

Slang and Jargon

Slang and Jargon – Lesson 1

II. MATCHING.

1. F. catheter or catheterization
2. D. atrial fibrillation
3. G. appendectomy or appendicitis
4. B. chemotherapy
5. I. alkaline phosphatase
6. A. cholecystectomy
7. H. bilirubin
8. J. capsules
9. C. complete blood count with differential
10. E. bicarbonate

Slang and Jargon – Lesson 2

II. MATCHING.

1. E. detoxification
2. D. eosinophils
3. H. examination
4. A. flexible sigmoidoscopy
5. J. echocardiogram
6. I. discontinue or discharge
7. C. digoxin or digitalis
8. F. JJ stent
9. B. dipyridamole sestamibi
10. G. hematocrit

Slang and Jargon – Lesson 3

II. MATCHING.

1. C. hepatitis
3. H. electrolytes
5. J. magnesium
7. D. hematology and oncology
9. B. potassium

2. E. Foley catheter
4. A. laceration
6. G. potassium chloride
8. I. lymphocytes
10. F. hydrochlorothiazide

Slang and Jargon – Lesson 4

II. MATCHING.

1. G. oxygen saturation
3. A. pathology
5. I. neuropsychiatric
7. D. micrograms
9. J. neurology or neurological

2. H. milligrams
4. B. nebulizers
6. C. medications
8. E. metastases
10. F. monocytes

Slang and Jargon – Lesson 5

II. MATCHING.

1. H. rehabilitation
3. B. psychology/psychiatry
5. E. saturation
7. C. postoperative
9. I. perforation

2. F. pulse oximetry
4. A. preoperative
6. G. prepared
8. D. regurgitation

Slang and Jargon – Lesson 6

II. MATCHING.

1. D. ventricular tachycardia
3. A. sedimentation rate
5. G. tablets
7. B. total bilirubin

2. F. vocational rehabilitation
4. E. segmented neutrophils
6. C. abdominal aortic aneurysm

Foreign Terms

Foreign Terms – Lesson 1

II. FILL IN THE BLANK.

1. cafe au lait spot OR cafe au lait
3. addendum
5. auris sinistra
7. coup
9. bruit(s) OR bruit

2. auris dextra
4. cul-de-sac
6. ad libitum
8. aures utrae

Foreign Terms – Lesson 2

II. FILL IN THE BLANK.

1. Gilbert disease
2. en masse
3. in situ
4. in toto
5. en bloc
6. in ano
7. in extremis

Foreign Terms – Lesson 3

II. FILL IN THE BLANK.

1. per
2. statim
3. peau d'orange
4. raphe
5. Virchow-Robin spaces
6. status quo
7. oculus dexter
8. oculus sinister
9. Raynaud phenomenon OR Raynaud disease
10. oculus uterque

Foreign Terms – Lesson 4

II. FILL IN THE BLANK.

1. hour
2. twice a day OR twice daily
3. by mouth
4. at bedtime OR hour of sleep
5. before food
6. day
7. a drop
8. in the morning

Foreign Terms – Lesson 5

II. FILL IN THE BLANK.

1. afternoon OR between noon and midnight
2. three times a day OR 3 times a day
3. as needed
4. four times a day OR 4 times a day
5. every two hours OR every 2 hours
6. every day
7. every hour
8. every

Word Differentiation

Word Differentiation – Lesson 1

I. MATCHING.

1. K. toward the center
2. A. a misleading image
3. F. expression of emotion
4. G. to leave out
5. L. an adenoma
6. J. the result or outcome
7. B. to agree to
8. E. the avoidance of
9. I. away from the center
10. C. disease of the glands
11. D. productive of results
12. H. arising from emotions

II. MULTIPLE CHOICE.

1. accept
2. affected
3. delusions
4. except
5. Effective
6. effects

7. afferent
9. adenocyst
11. affective

8. allusions
10. elusion
12. adenosis

Word Differentiation – Lesson 2

I. MATCHING.
1. H. serous fluid in the abdomen
3. A. line revolved about
5. D. wasting away
7. B. acid-forming
9. M. assisting device
11. L. pertaining to allergies
13. N. person who assists

2. I. involuntary discharge of urine
4. F. excision of arterial plaque
6. J. not poisonous
8. C. displaced
10. E. retention of urine
12. K. lacking strength
14. G. to get at

II. MULTIPLE CHOICE.
1. ascitic
3. enuresis
5. acidic
7. atherectomy
9. access
11. aid

2. arthrectomy
4. ectopic
6. anuresis
8. atony
10. atoxic

Word Differentiation – Lesson 3

I. MATCHING.
1. B. pertaining to the arm
3. A. pertaining to the ear
5. C. medicinal mass
7. I. pertaining to the mouth
9. G. resembling fish gills
11. D. hard

2. K. bulb-like
4. H. air passage in the lungs
6. J. localized hyperplasia of the epidermis
8. F. characterized by bullae
10. E. rounded enlargement

II. MULTIPLE CHOICE.
1. bolus
3. oral
5. brachial
7. callus
9. bulbus

2. branchial
4. bulbous
6. aural
8. bullous
10. bronchial

Word Differentiation – Lesson 4

I. MATCHING.
1. J. canal formation
3. H. direction of progress
5. C. milky fluid
7. F. cannula insertion
9. B. approximation

2. I. layer of grey matter
4. G. contraction
6. D. rough or harsh
8. E. near the ear
10. A. neck artery

II. MULTIPLE CHOICE.

1. coarse
2. canalization
3. parotid
4. claustrum
5. Carotid
6. cannulization
7. course
8. coaptation
9. colostrum
10. coarctation

Word Differentiation – Lesson 5

I. MATCHING.

1. B. beak-shaped
2. I. the heart
3. K. study of cells
4. A. flattering remark
5. H. center
6. J. moral indicator
7. D. coating of the eye
8. F. accessory
9. E. awake and alert
10. C. military division
11. G. knowledge of nutrition

II. MULTIPLE CHOICE.

1. Corps
2. complementary
3. coracoid
4. conscious
5. Cytology
6. compliments
7. core
8. choroid
9. COR
10. conscience

Word Differentiation – Lesson 6

I. MATCHING.

1. I. material for coloring
2. F. to draw out
3. H. abnormal development
4. G. illegal
5. J. repetition of sound
6. B. to stop living
7. E. impairment of speech
8. K. showing good judgment
9. A. difficulty swallowing
10. C. plural echocardiogram
11. D. individually distinct

II. MULTIPLE CHOICE.

1. discrete
2. elicit
3. dye
4. dysphagia
5. echos
6. illicit
7. die
8. dysphasia
9. echoes
10. discreet
11. dysplasia

Word Differentiation – Lesson 7

I. MATCHING.

1. H. increase of symptoms
2. D. closure of a wound
3. C. removal of a nerve
4. J. nerve distribution
5. F. excrement
6. B. being irritated
7. G. fibrous tissue
8. E. barium injection
9. I. expression of face
10. A. pertaining to the face

II. MULTIPLE CHOICE.

1. feces
2. enervation
3. fascial
4. exacerbation
5. enterocleisis
6. Innervation
7. facies
8. enteroclysis
9. exasperation
10. facial

Review: Lessons 1-7

I. MATCHING.

1. D. an adenoma in which there is cyst formation
2. B. any disease of the glands; abnormal development or formation of gland tissue
3. A. of or pertaining to an acid; acid-forming
4. G. pertaining to or characterized by ascites: the effusion and accumulation of serous fluid in the abdominal cavity
5. F. relating to the principal artery of the neck
6. H. situated or occuring near the ear, most commonly as in the parotid gland
7. E. aware of the moral right and wrong of one's actions
8. C. aware; mentally awake or alert

II. FILL IN THE BLANK.

1. discreet
2. echoes
3. islet
4. discrete
5. eyelet
6. echos

Word Differentiation – Lesson 8

I. MATCHING.

1. F. pertaining to excrement
2. D. at the bottom
3. H. albuminoid substance
4. I. sac in the spine
5. K. uniform quality
6. J. a bending
7. B. sharing an ancestor
8. E. a muscle flexing a joint
9. C. pertaining to the cecum
10. A. glassy or transparent
11. G. caused by a fungus

II. MULTIPLE CHOICE.

1. fundal
2. homogeneous
3. flexure
4. fecal
5. hyaline
6. thecal
7. Flexor
8. homogeneous
9. cecal
10. fungal

Word Differentiation – Lesson 9

I. MATCHING.

1. I. enter drop by drop
2. J. leading or bringing in
3. E. rounded process
4. G. to establish in place
5. H. within a cavity
6. B. hip bone
7. A. auditory ossicle
8. F. establishing anesthesia
9. D. portion of small intestine
10. C. within the eye

1. instillation
2. malleolus
3. ilium
4. induction
5. malleus
6. ileo-
7. installed
8. intralocular
9. introduction
10. intraocular

Word Differentiation – Lesson 10

I. MATCHING.

1. J. pertaining to a door
2. I. free slime
3. F. spread of disease
4. H. bony, osseous
5. G. resembling mucus
6. A. mediastinal operation
7. D. part of the long bone
8. E. cutting through the sternum
9. B. pertaining to the mind
10. C. a fold of the peritoneum (adj)

II. MULTIPLE CHOICE.

1. metaphysis
2. mucus
3. ostial
4. median sternotomy
5. mucous
6. mental
7. metastasis
8. osteal
9. mediastinotomy
10. omentum

Word Differentiation – Lesson 11

I. MATCHING.

1. D. simple
2. G. continue
3. I. serous membrane or abdomen
4. H. fibular
5. C. to go in front of
6. A. area between the thighs
7. J. a straight surface
8. E. injection by alternate route
9. F. pertaining to the perineum
10. B. pertaining to parents

II. MULIPLE CHOICE.

1. peritoneum
2. proceed
3. peroneal
4. plane
5. parenteral
6. plain
7. preceded
8. parental
9. perineum

Word Differentiation – Lesson 12

I. MATCHING.

1. B. male gland
2. E. abundance
3. M. vocal sound
4. I. pouring over or through
5. K. strictly regulated activity
6. C. involuntary action
7. H. where one lives
8. J. backward flow
9. D. lying horizontal
10. F. military unit
11. L. being thrust forward
12. G. artificial part
13. A. relating to a male gland

II. MULTIPLE CHOICE.

1. perfusion
2. regimen
3. prostate
4. reflexes
5. protrusion
6. prostrate

7. residents
9. resonance
11. prosthetic

8. prostatic
10. regiment
12. reflux

Word Differentiation – Lesson 13

I. MATCHING.

1. F. organic compound
3. J. not a real word
5. D. path
7. H. a region
9. B. nonmetallic element

2. G. seeing
4. C. a location
6. I. deep membranous layer
8. A. the lowermost portion
10. E. channel

II. MULTIPLE CHOICE.

1. route
3. Scarpa's
5. sight
7. tract
9. tracked

2. site
4. silicone
6. root
8. silicon

Word Differentiation – Lesson 14

I. MATCHING.

1. G. towards the tongue
3. C. hook-shaped (adj.)
5. K. thick and slow-flowing
7. A. between the chest and hips
9. F. gradual loss or decay
11. J. large organ

2. D. summit or top
4. E. used for ulcers
6. I. pertaining to the nails
8. B. used for anxiety
10. H. a whorled design

II. MULTIPLE CHOICE.

1. vortex
3. sublingually
5. wasting
7. subungual
9. uncal
11. viscous

2. Zantac
4. vertex
6. Xanax
8. waist
10. viscus

Review: Lessons 8-14

I. MATCHING.

1. I. those who live in a place; physicians serving in residency
3. D. pertaining to or towards the tongue
5. H. bony, osseous
7. B. pertaining to the uncus

9. J. the prolongation and intensification of sound produced by the transmission of its vibrations to a cavity

2. C. pertaining to an ostium (a door or opening)
4. G. the place where one lives
6. A. extended in a horizontal position
8. E. a gland in the male that surrounds the neck of the bladder and the urethra
10. F. pertaining to the nails (fingernails and toenails)

II. MULTIPLE CHOICE.

1. site
2. tracked
3. homogenous
4. track
5. sight
6. malleus
7. malleolus
8. tract
9. preceded
10. homogeneous

Abbreviations

Physical Examination – Lesson 1

II. FILL IN THE BLANK.

1. BP
2. CNS
3. A&P
4. CCE
5. CVA

III. FILL IN THE BLANK.

1. blood pressure
2. clubbing, cyanosis, or edema
3. auscultation and percussion
4. costovertebral angle
5. central nervous system

Physical Examination – Lesson 2

II. FILL IN THE BLANK.

1. GI
2. EOMI
3. DTRs
4. JVD
5. HEENT
6. IAC
7. GU

III. FILL IN THE BLANK.

1. jugular venous distention
2. genitourinary
3. Head, eyes, ears, nose and throat
4. Deep tendon reflexes
5. Extraocular muscles intact
6. gastrointestinal
7. internal auditory canal

Physical Examination – Lesson 3

II. FILL IN THE BLANK.

1. OD
2. NAD
3. JVP
4. OS
5. NC/AT

III. FILL IN THE BLANK.

1. no acute distress
2. right eye
3. left eye
4. normocephalic, atraumatic
5. jugular venous pressure

Physical Examination – Lesson 4

II. FILL IN THE BLANK.
1. PERRLA
2. TM
3. PMI
4. REM
5. ROM

III. FILL IN THE BLANK.
1. tympanic membrane
2. range of motion
3. pupils equal, round, reactive to light and accommodation
4. rapid eye movement
5. point of maximal impulse

Review: Physical Examination

I. FILL IN THE BLANK.
1. IAC
2. clubbing, cyanosis, or edema
3. PMI
4. EOMI
5. tympanic membrane
6. GU
7. no acute distress
8. OS
9. head, eyes, ears, nose and throat
10. range of motion

II. MULTIPLE CHOICE.
1. A&P
2. CVA
3. IAC
4. GI
5. DTR
6. NC/AT
7. REM
8. OD

Laboratory Data – Lesson 1

II. FILL IN THE BLANK.
1. ABGs
2. AFB
3. BUN
4. CBC
5. CO2
6. C&S

III. FILL IN THE BLANK.
1. carbon dioxide
2. blood urea nitrogen
3. complete blood count
4. arterial blood gas
5. culture and sensitivity
6. acid-fast bacillus

Laboratory Data – Lesson 2

II. FILL IN THE BLANK.
1. CSF
2. FEV
3. FVC
4. GTT
5. H&H
6. HIV
7. KCl
8. LFTs

III. FILL IN THE BLANK.
1. liver function tests
2. hemoglobin and hematocrit
3. human immunodeficiency virus
4. cerebrospinal fluid
5. forced vital capacity
6. glucose tolerance test
7. potassium chloride

Laboratory Data – Lesson 3

II. FILL IN THE BLANK.
1. PFTs
3. LP
5. PTT

2. PT
4. PSA
6. O&P

III. FILL IN THE BLANK.
1. prothrombin time
3. lumbar puncture
5. pulmonary function tests

2. partial thromboplastin time
4. ova and parasites
6. prostate-specific antigen

Laboratory Data – Lesson 4

II. FILL IN THE BLANK.
1. RBC
3. SMA
5. UA
7. WBCs

2. RPR
4. TB
6. WBC
8. RBCs

III. FILL IN THE BLANK.
1. white blood cells
3. red blood cells
5. rapid plasma reagin
7. white blood cells

2. tuberculosis
4. urinalysis
6. simultaneous multichannel autoanalyzer
8. red blood cells

Review: Laboratory Data

I. FILL IN THE BLANK.
1. C&S
3. blood urea nitrogen
5. complete blood count
7. HIV
9. LFT

2. prothrombin time
4. CO2
6. FVC
8. arterial blood gas
10. glucose tolerance test

II. MULTIPLE CHOICE.
1. H&H
3. PSA
5. FEV
7. PTT

2. KCl
4. O&P
6. AFB
8. CSF

Diseases and Syndromes – Lesson 1

II. FILL IN THE BLANK.
1. respiratory
3. acquired
5. hypertrophy
7. aneurysm

2. syndrome
4. deficiency
6. lymphocytic OR lymphoblastic

1. benign prostatic hypertrophy OR benign prostatic hyperplasia
2. acquired immune deficiency syndrome OR acquired immunodeficiency syndrome
3. abdominal aortic aneurysm
4. acute lymphocytic leukemia OR acute lymphoblastic leukemia
5. adult respiratory distress syndrome

Diseases and Syndromes – Lesson 2

II. FILL IN THE BLANK.

1. carcinoma OR cancer
2. chronic obstructive
3. congestive
4. cystic
5. cerebrovascular
6. megalovirus

III. FILL IN THE BLANK.

1. cytomegalovirus
2. chronic obstructive pulmonary disease
3. congestive heart failure
4. carcinoma (cancer) OR cancer (carcinoma)
5. cerebrovascular accident
6. cystic fibrosis

Diseases and Syndromes – Lesson 3

II. FILL IN THE BLANK.

1. idiopathic
2. hyperostosis
3. thrombosis
4. Fibrocystic
5. mellitus
6. degenerative

III. FILL IN THE BLANK.

1. deep venous thrombosis OR deep vein thrombosis
2. diabetes mellitus
3. degenerative joint disease
4. diffuse idiopathic skeletal hyperostosis
5. fibrocystic disease

Diseases and Syndromes – Lesson 4

II. FILL IN THE BLANK.

1. reflux
2. herniated
3. pulposus
4. interstitial
5. insulin-dependent
6. hyaline

III. FILL IN THE BLANK.

1. hyaline membrane disease
2. gastroesophageal reflux disease
3. insulin-dependent diabetes mellitus
4. herniated nucleus pulposus
5. interstitial lung disease

Diseases and Syndromes – Lesson 5

II. FILL IN THE BLANK.

1. sclerosis
2. rheumatoid
3. dystrophy
4. syncytial
5. post-traumatic

III. FILL IN THE BLANK.

1. multiple sclerosis
2. post-traumatic stress disorder
3. respiratory syncytial virus
4. rheumatoid arthritis
5. reflex sympathetic dystrophy

Diseases and Syndromes – Lesson 6

II. FILL IN THE BLANK.

1. respiratory
2. systemic
3. erythematosus
4. ischemic attack
5. urinary
6. infection
7. sudden
8. syndrome

III. FILL IN THE BLANK.

1. transient ischemic attack
2. urinary tract infection
3. systemic lupus erythematosus
4. upper respiratory infection
5. sudden infant death syndrome

Review: Diseases and Syndromes

I. FILL IN THE BLANK.

1. joint
2. cerebro
3. obstructive pulmonary
4. death syndrome
5. transient
6. failure
7. respiratory
8. venous thrombosis
9. urinary
10. idiopathic skeletal

II. MATCHING.

1. G. infection
2. H. arthritis
3. A. cytomegalo
4. F. mellitus
5. J. membrane
6. B. syncytial
7. I. stress
8. C. thrombosis
9. D. carcinoma
10. E. transient

III. MULTIPLE CHOICE.

1. erythematosus
2. cystic
3. sympathetic
4. pulposus
5. reflux
6. interstitial
7. congestive
8. disease
9. multiple
10. cystic

Surgery – Lesson 1

II. FILL IN THE BLANK.

1. amputation
2. tunnel
3. esophagogastroduodenoscopy
4. Estimated
5. knee

III. FILL IN THE BLANK.

1. estimated blood loss
2. above-knee amputation
3. below-knee amputation
4. carpal tunnel release
5. esophagogastroduodenoscopy

Surgery – Lesson 2

II. FILL IN THE BLANK.

1. intra
2. muscular OR venous
3. endotracheal
4. jugular
5. incision
6. drainage

III. FILL IN THE BLANK.

1. intravenous
2. endotracheal
3. intramuscular
4. incision and drainage
5. internal jugular

Surgery – Lesson 3

II. FILL IN THE BLANK.

1. reduction
2. fixation
3. nasogastric
4. Kirschner
5. laparoscopic
6. Ringer's

III. FILL IN THE BLANK.

1. nasogastric
2. open reduction, internal fixation
3. lactated Ringer's
4. Kirschner wire
5. laparotomy OR laparoscopic

Surgery – Lesson 4

II. FILL IN THE BLANK.

1. arthroplasty
2. Transurethral
3. Swan-Ganz
4. resection
5. hip OR knee
6. adenoidectomy

III. FILL IN THE BLANK.

1. total hip arthroplasty
2. transurethral resection of the bladder tumor
3. Swan-Ganz
4. total knee arthroplasty
5. transurethral resection of the prostate
6. tonsillectomy and adenoidectomy

Review: Surgery

I. FILL IN THE BLANK.

1. drainage
2. Ganz
3. amputation
4. Below
5. tracheal
6. Estimated
7. arthroplasty
8. Kirschner
9. intra
10. venous

II. MATCHING.

1. E. total
2. B. transurethral
3. H. gastric
4. A. tonsillectomy
5. G. reduction
6. D. muscular
7. F. incision
8. C. duodenoscopy
9. I. tumor
10. J. laparotomy

Radiology – Lesson 1

II. FILL IN THE BLANK.
1. posterior
2. encephalogram
3. gastrointestinal OR GI
4. Computed
5. cholangiopancreatography
6. Barium

III. FILL IN THE BLANK.
1. endoscopic retrograde cholangiopancreatography
2. barium enema
3. computed tomography
4. electroencephalogram
5. gastrointestinal
6. anteroposterior/posteroanterior

Radiology – Lesson 2

II. FILL IN THE BLANK.
1. hydroxyiminodiacetic
2. Intravenous
3. kidneys
4. bladder
5. gated acquisition
6. Magnetic
7. cholecystogram
8. cystourethrogram

III. FILL IN THE BLANK.
1. multiple gated acquisition
2. intravenous pyelogram
3. magnetic resonance imaging
4. hydroxyiminodiacetic acid OR hydroxy-iminodiacetic acid
5. kidneys, ureters, bladder
6. voiding cystourethrogram
7. oral cholecystogram

Review: Radiology

I. FILL IN THE BLANK.
1. posterior
2. Oral
3. gated acquisition
4. retrograde cholangiopancreatography
5. gastrointestinal
6. Electro
7. ureters
8. Computed
9. Voiding
10. Magnetic
11. imaging
12. iminodiacetic
13. pyelogram
14. enema

II. MULTIPLE CHOICE.
1. electroencephalogram
2. barium enema
3. posteroanterior
4. intravenous pyelogram
5. magnetic resonance imaging
6. gastrointestinal
7. computed tomography
8. kidneys, ureters, bladder
9. oral cholecystogram
10. multiple gated acquisition

Cardiology – Lesson 1

II. FILL IN THE BLANK.
1. fibrillation
2. arteriosclerotic OR atherosclerotic
3. cardiac
4. arteriosclerotic OR atherosclerotic
5. ventricular
6. vascular

III. FILL IN THE BLANK.

1. arteriosclerotic coronary artery disease OR atherosclerotic coronary artery disease
2. arteriosclerotic cardiovascular disease OR atherosclerotic cardiovascular disease
3. atrioventricular
4. atrial fibrillation
5. arteriosclerotic heart disease OR atherosclerotic heart disease
6. advanced cardiac life support

Cardiology – Lesson 2

II. FILL IN THE BLANK.

1. fem
2. artery
3. grafting
4. ejection
5. electrocardio
6. fem-fem OR fem-pop

III. FILL IN THE BLANK.

1. ejection fraction
2. coronary artery bypass grafting
3. femoral-femoral
4. femoral-popliteal
5. electrocardiogram

Cardiology – Lesson 3

II. FILL IN THE BLANK.

1. anterior
2. left
3. mammary
4. inferior
5. cava
6. oblique
7. coronary OR circumflex

III. FILL IN THE BLANK.

1. left circumflex artery OR left coronary artery
2. left internal mammary artery
3. inferior vena cava
4. left anterior oblique
5. left anterior descending

Cardiology – Lesson 4

II. FILL IN THE BLANK.

1. ventricular contraction
2. Myocardial
3. obtuse
4. percutaneous transluminal
5. angioplasty
6. ventricular
7. embolism OR embolus
8. patent ductus
9. descending
10. Peripheral

III. FILL IN THE BLANK.

1. obtuse marginal branch
2. left ventricle OR left ventricular
3. premature ventricular contraction
4. myocardial infarction
5. percutaneous transluminal coronary angioplasty
6. patent ductus arteriosus OR posterior descending artery
7. pulmonary embolism OR pulmonary embolus
8. peripheral vascular disease

Cardiology – Lesson 5

II. FILL IN THE BLANK.

1. anterior
2. coronary OR circumflex
3. ventricular
4. vena cava
5. descending
6. mesenteric

III. FILL IN THE BLANK.

1. ventricular tachycardia
2. superior vena cava
3. right anterior descending
4. right coronary artery OR right circumflex artery
5. right anterior oblique
6. superior mesenteric artery

Review: Cardiology

I. FILL IN THE BLANK.

1. ventricular
2. tachycardia
3. anterior
4. vena
5. arteriosus
6. descending
7. vascular
8. mammary
9. superior
10. myocardial

II. MATCHING.

1. C. ventricular
2. D. grafting
3. H. transluminal
4. A. ejection
5. J. circumflex
6. E. embolism
7. F. mesenteric
8. B. oblique
9. I. atherosclerotic
10. G. left

III. MULTIPLE CHOICE.

1. left ventricle
2. obtuse marginal branch
3. patent ductus arteriosus
4. peripheral vascular disease
5. femoral-popliteal
6. arteriosclerotic coronary artery disease
7. atrial fibrillation
8. advanced cardiac life support
9. inferior vena cava
10. myocardial infarction

Fetal Measurements – Lesson 1

II. FILL IN THE BLANK.

1. biparietal diameter
2. femur length
3. estimated fetal weight
4. abdominal circumference
5. head circumference

General History – Lesson 2

II. FILL IN THE BLANK.

1. gravida
2. abortion OR abortus
3. spontaneous abortion
4. para
5. therapeutic abortion

Obstetrical Terms – Lesson 3

II. FILL IN THE BLANK.

1. cesarean
2. confinement
3. intrauterine
4. retardation
5. cephalopelvic
6. estimated

Obstetrical Terms – Lesson 4

II. FILL IN THE BLANK.

1. menstrual
2. spontaneous
3. gestational
4. alpha fetoprotein
5. vaginal birth
6. rupture
7. delivery

III. FILL IN THE BLANK.

1. large for gestational age
2. cesarean section
3. last menstrual period
4. cephalopelvic disproportion
5. maternal serum alpha fetoprotein OR maternal serum alpha-fetoprotein
6. intrauterine growth retardation
7. estimated date of confinement
8. estimated gestational age
9. rupture of membranes
10. normal spontaneous vaginal delivery
11. vaginal birth after cesarean
12. labor and delivery

Gynecology Terms – Lesson 5

II. FILL IN THE BLANK.

1. inflammatory
2. salpingo
3. hysterectomy
4. vaginal OR abdominal
5. curettage

III. FILL IN THE BLANK.

1. total abdominal hysterectomy, bilateral salpingo-oophorectomy OR total abdominal hysterectomy and bilateral salpingo-oophorectomy
2. total vaginal hysterectomy
3. dilatation and curettage OR dilation and curettage
4. pelvic inflammatory disease
5. bilateral salpingo-oophorectomy

Review: Obstetrics and Gynecology

I. FILL IN THE BLANK.

1. circumference
2. disproportion
3. inflammatory
4. abortion
5. Estimated
6. period
7. growth
8. hysterectomy
9. Femur
10. oophorectomy

II. MULTIPLE CHOICE.

1. cephalopelvic
2. therapeutic
3. abdominal
4. confinement
5. gestational
6. cesarean
7. alpha
8. femur
9. estimated
10. head

1. D. spontaneous
2. C. gravida
3. A. diameter
4. B. membrane
5. F. dilatation
6. I. para
7. H. vaginal
8. J. inflammatory
9. G. delivery
10. E. intrauterine

Orthopedics – Lesson 1

II. FILL IN THE BLANK.

1. clavicular
2. cruciate
3. cervical
4. carpo
5. interphalangeal
6. orthosis OR orthotic
7. degenerative

III. FILL IN THE BLANK.

1. distal interphalangeal
2. acromioclavicular
3. carpometacarpal
4. cervical spine
5. anterior cruciate ligament
6. ankle-foot orthosis OR ankle-foot orthotic
7. degenerative disc disease

Orthopedics – Lesson 2

II. FILL IN THE BLANK.

1. iliotibial
2. metacarpo (or inter) OR inter (or metacarpo)
3. sacral
4. phalangeal
5. lumbar
6. collateral

III. FILL IN THE BLANK.

1. metacarpophalangeal
2. lumbar spine
3. interphalangeal
4. lumbosacral
5. iliotibial
6. medial collateral ligament

Orthopedics – Lesson 3

II. FILL IN THE BLANK.

1. posterior
2. temporo
3. Sacro
4. thoracic OR T-
5. proximal
6. metatarso
7. fibular

III. FILL IN THE BLANK.

1. metatarsophalangeal
2. sacroiliac
3. thoracic spine
4. temporomandibular joint
5. posterior cruciate ligament
6. proximal interphalangeal
7. tibial-fibular OR tibiofibular

Review: Orthopedics

I. FILL IN THE BLANK.

1. fibular
2. clavicular
3. disc
4. sacral
5. Carpometa
6. tibial
7. collateral
8. orthosis
9. cruciate
10. interphalangeal

II. MATCHING.

1. D. sacro
2. C. phalangeal
3. A. temporomandibular
4. G. lumbar
5. C. phalangeal
6. B. cruciate ligament
7. H. interphalangeal
8. F. cervical
9. C. phalangeal
10. I. thoracic

III. MULTIPLE CHOICE.

1. ankle-foot orthosis
2. distal interphalangeal
3. lumbosacral
4. acromioclavicular
5. degenerative disc disease
6. posterior cruciate ligament
7. iliotibial
8. temporomandibular joint
9. proximal interphalangeal
10. carpometacarpal

Miscellaneous Abbreviations – Lesson 1

II. FILL IN THE BLANK.

1. against
2. advice
3. Dietetic
4. activities
5. Arteriovenous
6. Cardiopulmonary
7. lymphocytic
8. acetylsalicylic
9. positive airway

III. FILL IN THE BLANK.

1. against medical advice OR American Medical Association
2. cardiopulmonary resuscitation
3. American Dietetic Association
4. arteriovenous malformation
5. activities of daily living
6. acetylsalicylic acid
7. chronic lymphocytic leukemia

Miscellaneous Abbreviations – Lesson 2

II. FILL IN THE BLANK.

1. extracorporeal
2. lithotripsy
3. discontinued
4. RESUSCITATE
5. birth
6. delirium

III. FILL IN THE BLANK.

1. delirium tremens
2. DO NOT RESUSCITATE
3. discontinue or discharge OR discharge or discontinue
4. date of birth
5. extracorporeal shock-wave lithotripsy

Miscellaneous Abbreviations – Lesson 3

II. FILL IN THE BLANK.
1. History
2. gastroesophageal
3. hydrochlorothiazide
4. physical

III. FILL IN THE BLANK.
1. history of present illness
2. gastroesophageal
3. hydrochlorothiazide
4. history and physical

Miscellaneous Abbreviations – Lesson 4

II. FILL IN THE BLANK.
1. dose inhaler
2. thrombocytopenic
3. no known drug
4. consciousness
5. lower lobe
6. intraocular

III. FILL IN THE BLANK.
1. loss of consciousness
2. intraocular lens
3. no known drug allergies
4. left lower lobe
5. metered dose inhaler
6. idiopathic thrombocytopenic purpura

Miscellaneous Abbreviations – Lesson 5

II. FILL IN THE BLANK.
1. subcutaneously (subq) OR subcutaneously
2. parenteral
3. shortness
4. nothing
5. paroxysmal
6. dyspnea
7. fenfluramine

III. FILL IN THE BLANK.
1. nothing by mouth
2. shortness of breath
3. total parenteral nutrition
4. subcutaneous, subcutaneously OR subcutaneously
5. paroxysmal nocturnal dyspnea
6. phentermine-fenfluramine OR phentermine and fenfluramine

Review: Miscellaneous Abbreviations

I. FILL IN THE BLANK.
1. advice
2. Metered
3. birth
4. parenteral nutrition
5. Activities
6. Left lower
7. consciousness
8. Shortness
9. resuscitation
10. continue

II. MATCHING.
1. E. paroxysmal
2. J. allergies
3. B. tremens
4. C. airway
5. A. lymphocytic
6. H. extracorporeal
7. F. chlorothiazide
8. I. illness
9. D. acetylsalicylic
10. G. ocular

III. MULTIPLE CHOICE.

1. Dietetic
2. arteriovenous
3. purpura
4. lymphocytic
5. breath
6. metered
7. living
8. discontinue
9. lobe
10. parenteral